THE
ABSOLUTELY ESSENTIAL
GUIDE TO
WINTER PARK

The Village in the Heart of Central Florida

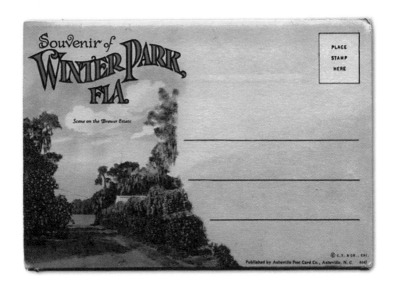

THE ABSOLUTELY ESSENTIAL COMPANY
WINTER PARK, FLORIDA
OCTOBER 2001

HAND-COLORED
POST CARD

Photographed and Published by Bowart.

THE ABSOLUTELY ESSENTIAL COMPANY
Post Office Box 1492
Winter Park, Florida 32790-1492

rchaps@msn.com

THIS SPACE FOR MESSAGE.   THIS SPACE FOR ADDRESS.

© 2001 by Robin Chapman
Library of Congress Control Number: 2001118897
ISBN Number 0-9714156-0-9

First Printing October 2001
Second Printing August 2002

THE
ABSOLUTELY ESSENTIAL
GUIDE TO
WINTER PARK

The Village in the Heart of Central Florida

BY
ROBIN CHAPMAN

Greetings from WINTER PARK Florida

Illustrated with a collection of more than one hundred
historic postcards and archival photographs.

These motor courts on Route 17-92 are no longer around but
they are recalled in these postcards from half a century ago.

For My Family:
Mom, Dad, and Kimmy
With love and thanks

Wright's Motor Lodge — WINTER P.

2-19-51

Dear Ruth + Carl,
This is sure the
life and I am really
enjoying it. Would hate
to come back to the
winter you have been
having so far. Wish you
were here.

CONTENTS

Seminole Hotel from Lake Osceola.

Winter Park has been a winter resort since the day it was founded, as you will learn in this book, so it has hosted quite a few vacationers over the years. What is one of the things people do on vacation, besides relax? They send postcards to their families and friends, especially if they themselves are in the sunshine and their families and friends are not, to let them know that they are "having wonderful time" and "wish you were here." Which leads me to the postcards used in this book. Many of them are more than a century old, and I've used them to show Winter Park through the years in as many places as possible. Each postcard says a lot about Winter Park and Florida history, from the pictures people have chosen to send, to the postcards that companies have chosen to produce through the years. These postcards are little pieces of our culture as well as examples of visual art and slices of our history. I hope you enjoy them as much as I have. My grateful thanks to Mr. Rick Frazee and Mr. Russell Hughes for loaning me cards from their collections.

WELCOME TO WINTER PARK

"There may be on this continent, a village more beautiful than Winter Park, but if so I've never seen it." Irving Bachellor 1917

I discovered Winter Park in September 1989 when I came to Central Florida for a job interview. The company booked me into the Park Plaza Hotel, and when I stepped out onto the veranda of my room on that sultry night and surveyed Park Avenue, I felt certain I had come to Winter Park to stay. I loved the way Winter Park looked. I loved the train station in the center of town, the park, the brick streets, and the old buildings. It wasn't hard to imagine this little village a century ago when people had come here from the North, attracted by Florida's lush environment, its clean air, and its warm winter days.

In the late 19th century and the first years of the 20th, before the dawn of air-conditioning, many of the city's residents lived here only in the winter: hence the city's name, "Winter Park." Through some planning and some luck, much of Winter Park's early charm has been retained. And therein lies the attraction.

Now more than a million visitors a year come to Winter Park to enjoy its Farmers Market, its museums, its annual Art Festivals, to take The Winter Park Scenic Boat Tour, to stroll Park Avenue, and to visit Rollins College.

Within these pages, you'll find even more things that will keep you and your family busy on your visit to Winter Park.

A Winter Park postcard sold in the decade after World War II.
"The Colony" was where Winter Park went to the movies.

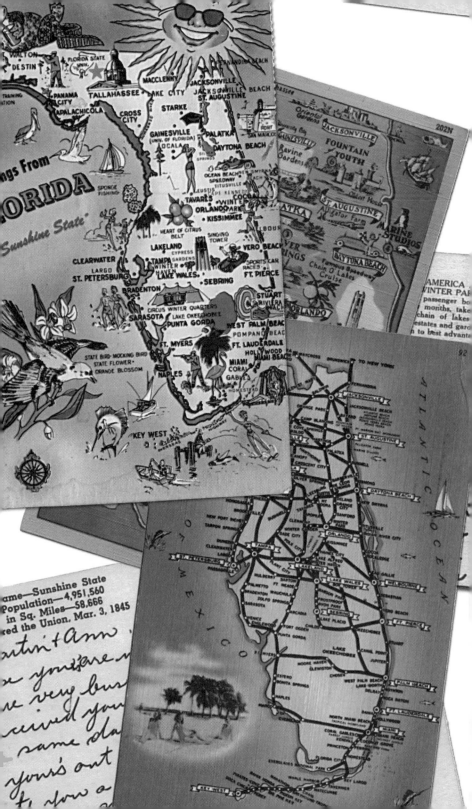

GETTING STARTED

This is a 1939 postcard of the Scenic Boat Tour.
Look at that boat!

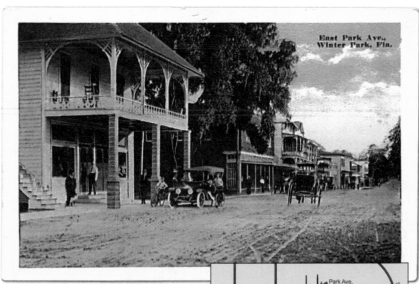

East Park Ave.,
Winter Park, Fla.

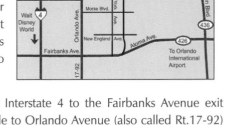

Clearly, if you're already in Winter Park, you can skip this page. But you might need these directions to share with your friends—or to return, which we hope you will.

"WISH YOU WERE HERE..." From Interstate 4 to the Fairbanks Avenue exit (Exit 45): take Fairbanks east one mile to Orlando Avenue (also called Rt.17-92) and turn left at the light. You'll be headed north. Go two blocks to Morse Boulevard and turn right. Travel almost one mile on Morse to New York Avenue. There are free parking lots at Morse and New York on both sides of the street. Park Avenue is just one block to the east.

THAT "SINKING" FEELING If the unusual interests you, there is something on your way to Park Avenue you won't want to miss. Exit I-4 at Fairbanks as above and drive east. When you get to Orlando Avenue (Rt.17-92), continue on Fairbanks to Denning Drive. Turn left on Denning Drive and immediately look to your left. On the northwest corner of Denning at Fairbanks, you'll see a very large hole filled with water. This is the famous Winter Park Sinkhole, which in May 1981 engulfed a couple of houses, a Porsche garage (five cars fell in), and a portion of the road you are sitting on now (which has since been repaired). The sinkhole looked even bigger before it filled with water. Once you've gazed at it (without causing an accident behind you) continue on Denning to Morse Boulevard, and turn right (east) to parking lots and Park Avenue as above.

A FEW NOTES FOR DRIVERS

Winter Park, like every other city and town in America, has its quirks. Before you run smack dab into them, here are a few notes to assist the driver in the family.

A STREET BY ANY OTHER NAME   Fairbanks Avenue is the main east-west artery through Winter Park. Curiously, it is also known by at least five names in varying parts of its length. From I-4 past Park Avenue it is called Fairbanks. Briefly past Park Avenue it is called Osceola Avenue. Briefly past that it is called Brewer Avenue. And just a little past that, it is known as Aloma Avenue. To add to the confusion, it is also called State Road 426. To keep it simple, I often just call it Fairbanks.

THEY'VE GOT YOUR TICKET TO RIDE   I used to tell my friends that there should be a sign as you enter Winter Park: Welcome to Winter Park! Don't Shift Out of Second! (I admit this was 10 years ago, after my third speeding ticket.) The point is this: the posted speed limits are low in Winter Park, and Winter Park's finest strictly enforce them. If you don't want a ticket, go the speed limit even if people behind you are honking their horns. In any case, things have improved. In 1904 the speed limit in Winter Park for any motorized vehicle was 8 miles an hour.

EXCUSE ME... IS THIS A PARKING SPACE?   We could call the city "Winter Don't-Park," but we try not to dwell on our parking challenges. There is free parking in two lots at New York and Morse. There is a paid garage at Park and Lyman (this has the advantage of being covered). And there is two-hour parking all around downtown. If you leave your car parked more than two hours in a two-hour spot, you are likely to get a parking ticket. There is a parking patrol in Winter Park, and it is very thorough. If you spend a bundle at one of the stores on Park Avenue, and then find a ticket on your car, don't feel shy about asking the proprietor of the establishment if he or she will pay your ticket for you. It has been known to happen. Don't try this if you just stopped in for a pack of gum.

This postcard was mailed from Winter Park to Stoneham, Massachusetts in December 1957.

Interlachen Ave., Winter Park, Fla.—1

A 1920s postcard of Interlachen Avenue.

BRICK STREETS (BUMPY, BUT CHARMING AND PRACTICAL)   Winter Park's brick streets rank very high on its list of assets. The first brick street was installed in 1915 to replace an old lime and clay roadbed, as the automobile came into common use. It is worth noting that bricks were originally used for economic reasons, not for their charm: asphalt and concrete roads were considered more desirable, but bricks from Georgia were cheaper. Over the years, some of the busier brick streets have been re-paved with asphalt. But there are still six miles of the old brick streets in Winter Park today. Now, a location on a brick street can add to the value of a Winter Park home. The Enhancement Project on Park Avenue (1998-2000) was designed to remove the street's asphalt covering and replace it with brick. What do you suppose workers found when they pulled up the asphalt covering Park Avenue? They found the old bricks.

The nonmortared brick streets in Winter Park are much more environmentally friendly than are asphalt streets. The bricks mortared only with sand allow the heavy Florida rains to seep back into and replenish the water table. Water hitting asphalt streets creates flooding and often becomes polluted runoff, which must be treated before it can be reused.

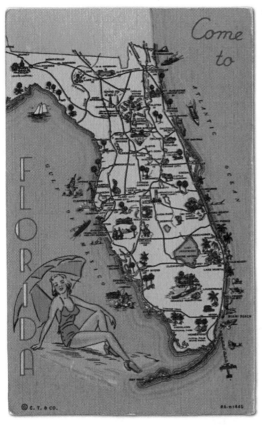

WEATHER Winter Park weather is consistently fine, which is one of the reasons so many people come here. Because it is a subtropical environment it has its share of rain, so an umbrella is always handy to have with you. When the summer thundershowers hit, you will want to use that umbrella to run for cover very quickly. Central Florida is also the lightning capital of the world!

Florida's beauty beckons in a mid-20th century postcard.

AVERAGE TEMPERATURE

	High		Low	
January	71°F	(21°C)	49°F	(9.4°C)
February	73°	(22)	50°	(10)
March	78°	(25)	55°	(12)
April	83°	(28)	59°	(15)
May	88°	(31)	66°	(19)
June	91°	(32)	72°	(22)
July	92°	(33)	73°	(23)
August	92°	(33)	73°	(23)
September	90°	(32)	72°	(22)
October	85°	(29)	66°	(19)
November	79°	(26)	58°	(14)
December	73°	(21)	51°	(10)

AVERAGE RAINFALL

	inches	(centimeters)
January	2.2	(5.5)
February	3.0	(7.6)
March	3.2	(8.1)
April	1.8	(4.5)
May	3.6	(9.1)
June	7.3	(18.5)
July	7.3	(18.5)
August	6.8	(17.2)
September	6.0	(15.2)
October	2.4	(6.0)
November	2.3	(5.8)
December	2.2	(5.5)

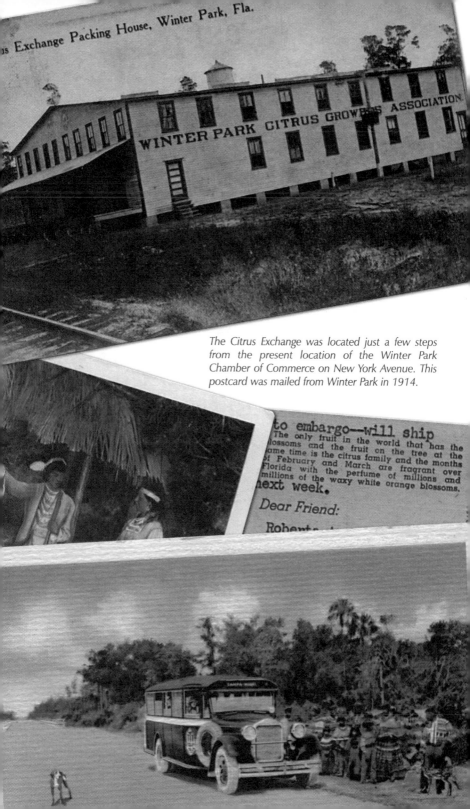

us Exchange Packing House, Winter Park, Fla.

WINTER PARK CITRUS GROWERS ASSOCIATION

The Citrus Exchange was located just a few steps from the present location of the Winter Park Chamber of Commerce on New York Avenue. This postcard was mailed from Winter Park in 1914.

to embargo—will ship
The only fruit in the world that has the blossoms and the fruit on the tree at the same time is the citrus family and the months of February and March are fragrant over Florida with the perfume of millions and millions of the waxy white orange blossoms, next week.

Dear Friend:

Roberts

Residence of E. H. Brewer, Winter Park, Fla.

This postcard (above) was postmarked May 17, 1911. In the 19th century, the house was home to Alonzo Rollins. The Brewers remodeled it extensively and it is today called "The Palms."

POST CARD

WINTER PARK, FL.

Post Card

MESSAGE

ORLANDO
OCT 6
1 PM
FLA.

Dear Ray

10-6-09

Mr. Ray Trovillo

Seminole Indians in the Heart of the Florida Everglades

A very collectible postcard of a scene in South Florida.

TIMUCUAN AND SEMINOLE

When the 16th century conquistadors gave La Florida its name ("place of flowers" in Spanish) thousands of native Americans of the Timucuan tribe were living in villages throughout Central Florida. Each tribe was independent, but they all shared the Maskoki (sometimes spelled Muskogee) language. The Spanish forced the Timucuan into mission villages, and in less than 200 years, war, intermarriage, disease, and hunger wiped them from the face of the earth. The last known Timucuan Indian, Juan Alonso Cabale, died in 1767.

In the early 19th century, members of native American tribes who had been driven from their traditional land on Florida's borders began to take refuge in Florida since it was then not a part of the United States. These people, some Creek, some Cherokee, some the vestiges of other tribes, banded together with runaway slaves and became a new tribe called the Seminoles. Osceola was one of their leaders. He was born in Alabama about 1802 of a Creek mother and a father who may or may not have been British. Raised as Billy Powell, he moved with his mother to Florida about 1814. He and his small band were very successful in their guerilla war against the U.S. government troops. Finally, a U.S. representative asked him to come in under the white flag to talk peace. When he did so, he was thrown into prison, first in St. Augustine and then near Charleston, where he died of malaria in 1838. By the 1850s, the Seminole Wars ended and the Seminoles who didn't agree to be relocated to Western reservations faded into the Everglades.

Some people believe that Osceola had a winter encampment along the eastern shore of Lake Osceola in what is now Winter Park—which explains the name of the lake. Settlers said there was an Indian trail along the lake, and early Winter Park residents celebrated "Osceola Day" in the chief's honor. Whether his presence is fact or myth, it is nice to imagine him in a rare peaceful moment, resting with his band of warriors and their families on the shore of this spring-fed lake.

In a way, the Seminoles have had their revenge. It wasn't until 1926 that the chief of the Seminoles wrote President Calvin Coolidge to say his people were finally ready to swear allegiance to the American flag. The Seminoles are now one of only two federally recognized native American tribes in Florida. They have organized a highly successful business in South Florida and are one of the wealthiest tribes in the United States.

Billy Bowlegs was a famous Seminole chief who died in 1864. This is a postcard of Billy Bowlegs III (1862-1965), a grandson of Osceola, who would have been in his forties when this postcard was made in the early 20th century. It was hand-colored by a Detroit Company.

This is an exceptionally beautiful early 20th century postcard, produced by the Hugh Leighton Company of Portland, Maine. It was hand colored in Germany.

A BRIEF LOOK AT WINTER PARK HISTORY

ettlers from the North began moving to Central Florida in the last third of the 19th century. A man named David Mizell arrived in what is now Winter Park from Alachua County in 1858. Two African Americans had early homesteads: Will Frazier in 1877 and Charles Williams possibly even earlier. It goes without saying that they all had to survive without bug spray and air-conditioning. Worse yet (or better yet, depending upon your point of view) as they followed an old trail to the shores of Lake Osceola, these hearty settlers saw no "civilization" for miles.

The real development began in 1881 with the arrival of Loring Chase. Born in Nashua, New Hampshire, he had spent most of his professional life in Illinois. He was a developer—as many Florida residents would be in the years to come. His idea was to start a town and build houses, which he could sell to wealthy people from the North. After nosing around a bit, he settled on a beautiful area filled with old pine trees, adjacent to a small chain of spring-fed lakes.

By then, a man named Wilson Phelps had settled in the area and had planted 1,400 orange trees, 150 lemon trees and 300 lime trees. In 1881, he wrote to Chase: *"You ask me to state frankly the drawbacks to a life in Florida in this vicinity and I will do so. In the first place in the summer there are mosquitoes, but they are no worse than they are in Illinois or New York. Of snakes we have some, but during my residence of seven years here in which I have been most of the time in the woods and fields, I have seen no more than I used to see in the fields of Illinois."*

Chase and his partner, Oliver Chapman, took Phelps' advice, bought 600 acres for the princely sum of $13,000, and laid out a city they called "Winter Park." It was Florida's first planned city. They set aside the land for what became Central Park and they laid out the long boulevard, which became Park Avenue.

Charles Hosmer Morse out for a spin with Mr. Temple, Mr. Brewer and Rollins President W.F. Blackman, in front of Rogers House. Mr. Brewer is at the wheel. Courtesy Department of College Archives and Special Collections, Olin Library, Rollins College.

Easy transportation to Florida helped their project. The railroad line between Sanford and Orlando was completed in 1881, and in 1882 Winter Park got its first train station. It sat just across the tracks from the present station.

Winter Park opened its first schools in 1883. In 1886 the first municipal election was held. One hundred and two voters were on the rolls when citizens approved Winter Park's incorporation as a town in 1887. (It wasn't until 1925 that it incorporated as a city.) One year later, a narrow-gauge rail line began operating between Winter Park and Orlando. Though the "Dinky Line" has long since vanished, a vestige of it remains in the "Dinky Dock" on Lake Virginia adjacent to Rollins College.

The decade of the 1880s was a boom time for Winter Park. Between 1880 and 1895, hundreds of acres of land were planted with citrus

The tracks of the narrow-gauge Orlando and Winter Park Railway–"The Dinky Line"–followed the shore of Lake Virginia. Courtesy Department of College Archives and Special Collections, Olin Library, Rollins College.

trees. Judge John R. Mizell, the son of pioneer David Mizell, had 3,000 trees on his 100 acres. As the turn of the century approached, there were still more trees than people: the full-time residents of Winter Park numbered no more than 600.

In 1885, leaders of the Congregational Church decided to establish an institution of higher education in the State of Florida. Winter Park residents made the most generous pledge, so the committee chose Winter Park as its home. Of those who gave to the college, Alonzo Rollins gave the most: $50,000, the equivalent of more than a million dollars today. He died two years later in Chicago, after having spent just a few years in Winter Park. But because of his generosity, Rollins College bears his name.

The first Rollins classes were held in the Congregational Church—then located just behind the present church fronting on Interlachen at New England Avenue. Within a year, Rollins had its first building and within four years, it had four more. Only one of the original buildings has survived: Pinehurst Hall, which is still in use.

In the late 19th century, the citrus industry was still very new in Florida. Growers had only a few decades' worth of experience with Florida winters, and they believed Winter Park was "below the frost line." In 1886 they got a warning, when a mild freeze killed all the fruit on the trees and ruined that year's crops. Then, in December 1894 and February 1895, Central Florida was hit with the coldest weather it would face for nearly a century. The killer freeze of the winter of 1894-1895 wiped out nearly every citrus tree in Central Florida. Many of the growers gave up and went home. It would be 25 years before the citrus industry in Central Florida would recover.

Winter Park still had its beauty, and visitors and new residents continued to come. The first golf course was built in 1899. (Grazing sheep were used to keep the greens trimmed.) During the next 30 years beautiful homes began to fill building lots throughout the city.

A photo taken in Central Florida after one of the coldest nights of the "great freeze"–December through February 1894-1895. Courtesy Department of College Archives and Special Collections, Olin Library, Rollins College.

Rollins students on a picnic at Lake Maitland, May 1891. Left to right: Adelle Swain, Arthur Brigham, Oliver Whitaker, Lois Parker, Minnie Forest, May Pomroy, Fred Swain, Frank Haynes, Emelie Hempel, Archie Shaw, Annie Fuller, Stewart Crawford, Sidney Williams, Eugenie Swain, Robert Benedict. Courtesy Department of College Archives and Special Collections, Olin Library, Rollins College.

Charles Hosmer Morse, a wealthy industrialist from Chicago, bought a winter home for himself and his family in 1904; he also bought out Chase and Chapman, purchasing hundreds of acres of land. His home, called "Osceola Lodge", can still be seen today on Interlachen Avenue. Morse was responsible for large donations of land and money, which gave Winter Park and Rollins College many of the features they have today. He was so beloved that when he lay dying in 1921 the city rerouted traffic near his home so he wouldn't be disturbed.

In the 1920s, Winter Park saw another spurt of growth. Though only a few of the homes built during the boom of the late 19th century survive,

Charles Hosmer Morse

many of those built in the 1920s do. On your visit, you'll see lots of examples of home styles popular in the 1920s: Arts and Crafts bungalows, Spanish Mediterranean, neo-Tudor, Georgian, and French Provincial homes abound in Winter Park's neighborhoods.

Winter Park is now a city of 25,000 residents on eight square miles of land, with 70 parks and 20,000 oak trees. The acres of citrus groves are gone—the victims of both frost and development. Yet they have left a legacy all their own. In almost every Winter Park garden there is a tree from one of the old groves. In the spring they still fill the air with the sweet scent of orange blossoms.

Early 20th century postcard.
There were no women in this family?

Rollins buildings haven't changed much in eighty years–but the cars certainly have.
Early 20th century postcard.

"As we rode along the lovely shores of Lakes Virginia, Osceola and Maitland, I was delighted, and having been in the real estate business for many years, had an eye for town sites, and built, not a castle in the air, but a town—never thinking it would materialize."
Loring Chase 1881

The Story of the Two Marys
NO MAN'S LAND

A mong the early settlers to the Winter Park area were Mary E. Brown (1822-1909) and her friend Mary McClure (1823-1895), who bought 10 acres from Wilson Phelps on Lake Sylvan and established their homestead about 1879. We know a little about their lives because Mary Brown kept regular diaries from 1876 through 1898, which are now part of the Winter Park Public Library's historical collection.

Mary Brown and Mary McClure in front of "No Man's Land" with Johnny Brown. Courtesy Department of College Archives and Special Collections, Olin Library, Rollins College, and the Winter Park Public Library.

The two spinsters had been teachers at Northwestern University in Evanston, Illinois and were in their late 50s when they began their pioneer adventure. In her brief but sometimes telling journal entries, Mary Brown emerges as a bundle of energy. On a typical day she records two or three changes in the weather and notes her daily activities, which include a whirlwind of hoeing, weeding, planting, driving to pick up the mail, loading fertilizer, paying calls on friends, going to church, and ironing. Sometimes she records the daily tragedies of life without comment, as she did on June 26, 1881: "Mr. Bigelow killed by lightning." And on March 15, 1898: "Sherman Copeland murdered his mistress last evening." Often she records something that might seem remarkable or exciting to us and buries it amidst the routine of her life, as she did in August of 1881: "Sowed onion seed, went to Phelps at 9:30 a.m. [*this seems to be where they picked up their mail,*] killed moccasin snake, M caught turtle [*M is her abbreviation for Mary McClure,*] thunder showers at noon." Sometimes, though rarely, she adds a revealing comment, as she did on New Year's Day of 1883: "Evening at Patchings—stupid." Later that month, she writes about a visit from some friends and adds: "ate too much." She appeared to be so busy, it's not surprising that on January 9,1882, she wrote: "Rain. Sick of overwork." In 1896, she made this unusual entry one March day: "Left off underwear." Several days later she wrote: "Resumed underwear." Considering the heavy clothing women wore at the time, and the Florida heat, modern women might find her decision completely understandable.

We can only speculate about what drove these two friends from Illinois to brave the hardships of a Florida homestead at the end of the 19th century. Mary Brown's father had been a missionary in St. Augustine and Jacksonville in the 1830s and it is possible Mary Brown fell in love with Florida as a child. The ladies left us, perhaps, a clue to their lives, when they named their homestead "No Man's Land." They did have one male in their lives: a donkey named Jack, whom Mary called "Johnny Brown" and whose adventures are often recorded in Mary Brown's diary, as in August 1881 when she notes after a particularly violent thunderstorm: "Jack trots home safe."

In addition to running their homestead, the two women became active in the community as it grew, establishing a school for African Americans on their property— that Mary Brown called "New Hope Cottage"—and serving on the early library and hospital boards.

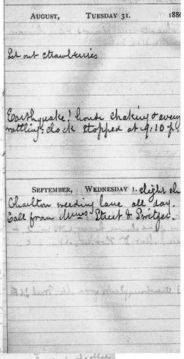

Original pages from the unpublished diary of Mary Brown. Courtesy of the Winter Park Public Library.

In December 1895 and January 1896 Mary's diary grows silent—which was very unusual for this prolific correspondent. Finally, on January 22 she notes going into Orlando and spending "$1.13 for veil." It was probably for her mourning clothes. Though it is not noted in the diary, Mary McClure died on December 29, 1895, at the age of 72. On February 5, Mary Brown records one of her most poignant entries: "Warm and bright. Home at 8. Put s.w. room in order, emptied the bureaus. Took down xmas hollies the last that Mary saw. She directed me how to put them over her mirror. Another last thing." Mary McClure's death continued to affect her. On February 8 she writes: "Threatening morning. Depressing day." And later in May she notes: "Painted chest, packed books, awful lonesome."

Within two years, Mary Brown had torn down the homestead and moved into town. At the age of 76, she built a house near the corner of Chase and Comstock. With her penchant for naming things she couldn't resist calling the new house— where she lived alone—"The Hermitage."

Mary Brown was one of the founding members of All Saints Episcopal Church, and in November 1891, she took part in the dedication of a stained glass memorial window honoring her father, the Rev. David Brown. When the old church building was torn down in 1945, the window was moved into the sacristy of the new church. It is now located with two other early windows in the men's vesting room of All Saints. It is believed the window was created in England. The inscription reads: "Rev. David Brown Born 1786 Died 1875 Missionary in East Florida 1833-1843 A Priest for 60 Years."

Mary Brown died in 1909 at the age of 87 and was buried in Winter Park's Palm Cemetery. In addition to her diaries, she left behind some of her recipes, of which there is more on the next few pages.

"No Man's Land" in the 1890s. The two Marys are in this picture, but you have to look closely to find them. One is sitting on the front porch. The other is sitting in front of the porch with a bowl in her lap. Courtesy Department of College Archives and Special Collections, Olin Library, Rollins College, and the Winter Park Library.

MARY BROWN'S RECIPES

Mary Brown's unpublished recipes are a part of the Winter Park Public Library's historical collection. As you can see, she did what many experienced cooks do: she jotted down a familiar recipe, and left no directions whatsoever.

MARY BROWN'S DOUGH CAKE

5 teacups dough

3 do sugar

2 do butter

5 eggs

1 tablespoon pearlash
(dissolved in a glass of wine)

This takes a little guesswork. Did she mean "dollop" where she wrote "do?" Pearlash was a commercial form of potassium carbonate, used in 19th-century recipes instead of yeast. You can actually order some online if you like. Or you could try using baking powder instead. By dough she might have meant sour dough, since it was the kind of thing one could keep around in those days without refrigeration.

Sausages
Dough Cake
5 teacups dough
5 eggs
dissolved in a glass of
Jumbles
roll them out
Bridge Port
Coffee Cup of Milk 6 Eggs
Fruit as you like

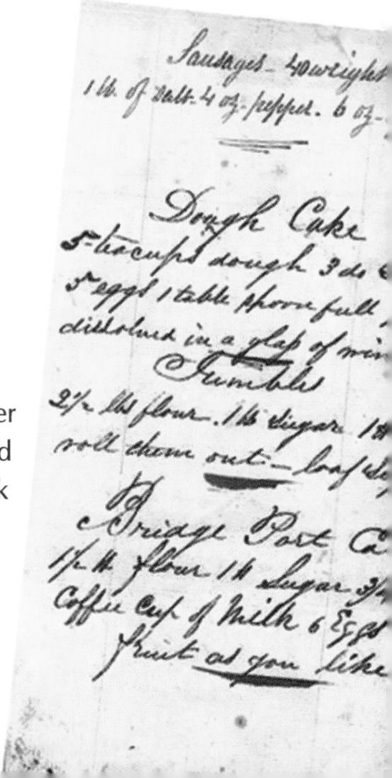

This is a modern recipe for sour dough:

4 cups flour

2 teaspoons salt

2 tablespoons sugar

Add: 3 to 4 cups potato water

Let stand loosely covered at 89°F
for about 2 days

You might try putting the sour dough with the other ingredients in a greased and floured cake pan, and cooking it at 375°F until it is done. Stick a toothpick in it, and if it comes out dry it is ready.

Original recipe notes in Mary Brown's handwriting. Courtesy of the Winter Park Library Collection.

MARY BROWN'S BRIDGE PORT CAKE

1½ cups flour

1 cup sugar

¾ cup butter

coffee cup of milk

6 eggs

fruit if you like

Once again, there are no directions. Try mixing the ingredients together, putting them in a greased and floured cake pan and cooking at 375°F until done. Then, try it with a cup of blueberries and see how it comes out. My sister tried this and said it resulted in something more like a puffy German pancake than a traditional cake.

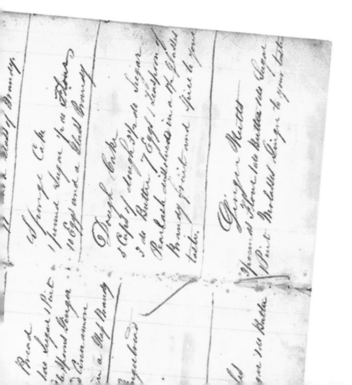

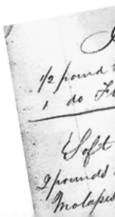

Most of the recipes Mary Brown saved were for sweets. Whether this indicates she had a sweet tooth, or just that she didn't need recipes for basic meat and potatoes is something we'll probably never know. This is one of several of her gingerbread recipes.

MARY BROWN'S SOFT GINGERBREAD

6 cups of flour

2 cups of molasses

1 cup of sugar

1 loaf of butter

3 eggs

1 cup of sour milk

2 teaspoons of saleratus

Does she mean a quarter pound of butter when she writes of "one loaf?" You'll have to try it. You may have to substitute yogurt or sour cream for the sour milk she calls for. Saleratus is an old-fashioned leavening that you can find on the Internet. Or you can try baking powder instead. How long to bake the gingerbread in how hot an oven? Think of it as your own pioneer experience.

HOTELS OF BYGONE DAYS

The developers of Winter Park in the 19th century planned the city as a winter resort so one of the first buildings they constructed was a hotel. Gradually over the decades, America's taste in resorts changed, and the old hotels were replaced by more modern ones. Yet the old hotels remain in the memories of many residents, and on the faces of old postcards from the past.

THE HOTEL WITH THREE NAMES The Virginia Inn, located on what is now the southeast corner of Morse and Interlachen, was the second building constructed in Winter Park. Opened in 1882 as Rogers House, it had a homey atmosphere and wonderful food that immediately attracted a loyal following. Charles Hosmer Morse, the millionaire who lived just up the street, said it was his favorite place to

eat in town. It began as a small resort with 30 rooms, and over the years, as it changed hands, it changed names and expanded in size. In 1904, a group of local businessmen—including Morse—bought it, renamed it The Seminole Inn, and gave it to Rollins College. In 1912 it was sold again, and for a while its new owner, Reuben Pratt Foley, just called it The Inn. In 1915, he renamed it The Virginia Inn, which it remained for the next half-century. Sunday dinner was served at noon, but it was Sunday supper, served in the evening, that both residents and visitors alike believed was its best meal. For 70 cents a diner was served a cold meat platter, salad, rolls, and homemade dessert. The small and select hotel attracted an elite clientele including President Chester A. Arthur in 1883, General and Mrs. Ulysses S. Grant, and, in 1962, Liberace.

In 1966 the Virginia Inn was sold for $235,000, and the building was razed to make room for The Cloisters Condominiums. The hotel's register and some of the artifacts that were saved from the building were given to the Rollins College archives.

Opposite page: Three postcards show the change of names of The Rogers House, to The Seminole Inn and then to The Virginia Inn. Note the ladder on the right side of the top postcard. Do you think they meant for that to be in the picture?

The Rogers House, Winter Park, Fla.

M.C.C

SEMINOLE INN, WINTER PARK, FLA.

Virginia Inn, Winter Park, Fla.—6

THE OLD SEMINOLE HOTEL The Old Seminole Hotel opened its doors on New Year's Day in 1886 and was for many years the largest hotel in the State of Florida. It was 293 feet long, could accommodate 400 guests, and featured steam heat, private baths, gas lighting, and an elevator. The Seminole was located on Lake Osceola at the eastern end of New England Avenue. Guests who looked out the windows of this five-story building could see 11 lakes, including Lake Osceola to the north and Lake Virginia to the south. During the 16 years it was in operation, its distinguished guests included President Grover Cleveland, Mrs. Benjamin Harrison, and the writer Harriet Beecher Stowe. Visitors arrived at the hotel on horse-drawn streetcars that ran up and down New England Avenue, traversing the half-mile from the railway station in just a few minutes.

Top: This envelope is from Seminole Hotel Stationery, postmarked 1888. Below: A very rare 1898 "postal card" of The Seminole Hotel which shows people, at left, playing tennis.

On September 18, 1902, a fire started in the Seminole's kitchen annex. The hotel was closed for the summer, and the only caretaker on the property didn't know how to operate the hotel's hoses. Word was sent to Orlando requesting help, but by the time Orlando firemen arrived, the hotel was completely engulfed in flames. The huge fire had attracted a crowd, and as the crowd realized the hotel was going to burn to the ground, there was some looting—liquor bottles and furniture were the primary targets. The only death occurred when a West Winter Park man named Albert Wilson, (some reports identify him as Talbot Wilson) who was helping to rescue furniture from the building, was trapped in the flames.

The hotel had cost a quarter of a million dollars to build, but it was insured for just $30,000, so the owners did not rebuild. Instead, they sold the property for building lots. Mrs. Ray Greene, the wife of one of Winter Park's mayors, grew up in a home on New England Avenue that was on the site of the Old Seminole Hotel. She later wrote that every time they dug in the garden they found debris from the old hotel, including broken dishes, a typewriter, and once, a room number tag.

A photo taken one week after The Seminole Hotel burned to the ground. The man in the picture may have been the caretaker of the hotel, who was awakened and rescued from the fire. Courtesy Department of College Archives and Special Collections, Olin Library, Rollins College.

Seminole Hotel, Winter Park, Fla.—5

There are hundreds of collectible postcards of The New Seminole Hotel which, for more than half a century, was the premier resort in Winter Park.

THE NEW SEMINOLE HOTEL Ten years after the Old Seminole Hotel burned to the ground, the owner of the Virginia Inn put together a company and built the New Seminole Hotel, which opened in 1913. It was located on five acres at the eastern end of Webster Avenue with 600 feet of frontage on Lake Osceola. For most of the 20th century it was a favorite resort of prominent visitors, including the Nobel laureate Sinclair Lewis. It had its own dock with room for private boats, and its guest rooms boasted the innovation of in-room telephones. The dining room at the New Seminole offered an 11-course dinner which, according to one old menu, included consommé, broiled salmon, ox tongue, rolls, roasted chicken, and pineapple soufflé pudding, capped by coffee and a variety of cheeses. In the late 1960s, the City of Winter Park voted against a plan to build condominiums on the site. In 1970 the hotel property was sold for $250,000, and the building was razed to make room for a cluster of lakefront homes. The houses on Kiwi Circle—each alone worth far more than the entire sale in 1970—now sit where the New Seminole Hotel once received its winter guests.

THE HOTEL ALABAMA The Hotel Alabama is the only one of the early Winter Park hotels to survive. It opened in 1922 on what had once been the estate of W.C. Temple on Lake Maitland. Guests approached The Alabama via its own drive, now called Alabama Drive, off Palmer Avenue. The hotel had four floors and 80 rooms so it was about halfway between The Virginia Inn and The New Seminole Hotel in size. When the train arrived in Winter Park from the North, the hotel's general manager would send to the station a hotel representative with a letter of introduction and a bevy of bellboys to assist his most valued incoming guests. In 1960, the hotel became The Mayell-Alabama Retirement Hotel. In 1979, it closed as a hotel, and re-opened in 1981 as a condominium property. As such it is still in operation today.

The Alabama no longer operates as a hotel, but it is little changed today from the day when hotel visitors sent these postcards to their friends up North.

The Langford Hotel in a 1950s postcard.

THE "OLD" LANGFORD The Langford Hotel was to the second half of the 20th century in Winter Park, what The Hotel Alabama, The New and Old Seminole Hotels, and The Virginia Inn were to the first half. Robert Langford was from a Chicago hotel family, and when he discovered Winter Park in the 1940s he believed it was on the verge of another development boom. Following World War II, he designed and constructed the Langford Hotel, which opened in January 1956. It was located at the corner of New England and Interlachen Avenues, just up the street from the earlier location of the Old Seminole Hotel. Once the Langford opened, everyone who was anyone who came to Central Florida from then on, stayed at the Langford including Ray Charles, Lillian Gish, Bob Dylan, Charleton Heston, President Ronald and First Lady Nancy Reagan (pre-White House), and The Platters, to name just a few of the celebrities who found a room at Mr. Langford's inn. The hotel was popular with locals too: residents who didn't have their own swimming pools joined The Langford pool in the summertime. The Langford closed May 30, 2000, and in March 2001, Robert Langford died at the age of 88. In the summer of 2001, plans were being developed to build a "New" Langford on the site of the old hotel.

WEST WINTER PARK

The neighborhood west of Central Park, sometimes called Hannibal Square or West Winter Park, is one of the oldest African American communities in the state. Nearby Eatonville, incorporated in 1883, counts itself as the oldest. West Winter Park was actually established two years earlier: it just never incorporated into its own city. Planned by Chase and Chapman when they built Winter Park, it was named after the legendary African general, Hannibal. As an African American neighborhood in a Florida resort town, it was a microcosm of the issues that faced the entire country 20 years after the Civil War and the Emancipation Proclamation.

"One quarter of a mile west from the depot is located Hannibal Square, designed for a church for colored people, and surrounding it, lots which will be sold to Negro families of good character." The South Florida Journal, 1881

Most—but not all—of the African American citizens who settled west of Central Park, worked for the residents who lived east of Central Park. They were the labor force in the groves, the homes, at the hotels, and on the estates of the city. Some African Americans ran their own businesses. Mr. I.W. Williams ran a grocery store. The second newspaper published in Winter Park was *The Advocate*, established in 1889. Mr. Gus Henderson was its publisher and Mr. S.A. Williams was its editor, and both men were from West Winter Park. For several years, after

West Winter Park's first school. Courtesy Department of College Archives and Special Collections, Olin Library, Rollins College.

Students with lunch pails, West Winter Park, 1907-1910. The picture was cut from a postcard and placed in a scrapbook which was bequeathed to Rollins College as part of the estate of alumna Agnes Clark Smith. Courtesy Department of College Archives and Special Collections, Olin Library, Rollins College.

Mr. Ghent and Mr. Larkin Franklin, caretaker and chauffeur of "Wheatlogue" in Winter Park, 1921. The photograph was part of the estate of Mrs. William Guild. Courtesy Department of College Archives and Special Collections, Olin Library, Rollins College.

The *Lochmede* folded on June 28, 1889, *The Advocate* was the only paper in town and covered news of general interest to everyone.

In 1886, six aldermen were elected to the council in Winter Park and two of them—Walter Simpson and Frank Israel—were African American men from the Hannibal Square neighborhood. Both Simpson and Israel served until 1893.

Things changed in 1893 when Democrats and Republicans in Winter Park disagreed over the future of Hannibal Square. The majority of Winter Park residents wanted to include West Winter Park in the city and refused to change its boundaries. But a minority in the city with powerful friends in the state legislature had the boundaries of Winter Park redrawn by state law, and West Winter Park was de-annexed. In 1925, the citizens appealed to the legislature again, and West Winter Park was re-annexed so that the town would be large enough to qualify as a city.

West Winter Park is home to two of the oldest churches in the city. The Mt. Moriah Baptist Church was founded in 1886 and its sanctuary was constructed in 1889. The Ward Chapel AME Church was founded in 1890 and its church building was constructed in 1893. Until they had their own buildings, the congregations of the two churches met on alternate Sundays at the Winter Park Town Hall.

Many of the families presently living in West Winter Park are the descendents of the first families who settled around Hannibal

The Mt. Moriah Missionary Baptist Church in West Winter Park, organized in 1886 by Reverend and Mrs. Charles Ambrose. The building was erected at the corner of Pennsylvania and Lyman Avenue in 1889. ©Peter Schreyer. This photograph and the photograph of Mr. and Mrs. Richmond J. Lawson (see page 35) are part of an award-winning photo study of West Winter Park made in 1994 by Peter Schreyer, Executive Director of the Crealdé School of Visual Art. The study was funded through a grant from The Winter Park Public Library and Rollins College Olin Library. The entire series may be viewed at The Winter Park Public Library.

Square. In recent years there has been a growing movement among them to record, preserve, treasure, and disseminate information about the historic neighborhood in which they live.

During the last decade of the 20th century, the neighborhood began to undergo many changes. Neighbors, Habitat for Humanity, and the City of Winter Park worked to repair, restore, and upgrade housing, razing buildings that could not be made to meet modern codes. Between 1991 and 1996, twenty-eight new affordable homes were constructed. A number of city businesses, crowded for space and concerned about escalating rents on Park Avenue, moved into the West Winter Park corridors of New England Avenue and Morse Boulevard, which are zoned for businesses.

Residents of West Winter Park have mixed feelings about the changes. They have long been part of a distinct and thriving community. They fear escalating land values will price many of their families out of their homes. While they welcome improvements in their streets, homes, and services, they believe their neighborhood should retain its own unique character.

How that should be done is of prime importance to the future of West Winter Park.

This is a postcard from Bamboo Groves which was on Morse Boulevard in Winter Park, telling the recipient that her Christmas basket of oranges is on its way. Bamboo Groves was owned by the Charles Wilsons, an African American family who lived in West Winter Park.

HISTORIC CEMETERIES

There are two historic cemeteries in Winter Park and both of them provide fascinating glimpses into the city's past.

The oldest cemetery, called Pineywood (it is sometimes called Pinewood and sometimes called Piney Wood in the old literature), was established between 1889 and 1890 and covers 12 acres on South Lakemont Avenue near Lake Baldwin. From 1889 through 1906 it was the only cemetery in Winter Park.

In 1906, the Palm Cemetery was established on two acres near the intersection of Webster and New York Avenues, closer to downtown Winter Park. Later, 14 more acres were added to the site. From then on, though no law has ever required this, African Americans were buried in Pineywood, and white residents were buried in Palm Cemetery.

On the southeast corner of Palm Cemetery, at the intersection of Webster and New York Avenues, you will find a tall marble memorial to Loring Chase (July 1, 1839-August 24, 1906), who with Oliver Chapman, was the founder of Winter Park. Chase was an anti-slavery Lincoln Republican from Illinois who made sure African Americans were included in every aspect of Winter Park life. Yet it was he who donated the first acreage for the Palm Cemetery, and thus it is one of history's unusual twists that he is buried in a segregated cemetery. Over the years his memorial has been replaced several times; consequently the present one does not date from the period of his death.

You could easily spend hours walking through both of these cemeteries. You will see many family names from Winter Park's history.

Loring Chase, one of the founders of Winter Park, died in 1906 and was one of the first Winter Park citizens to be buried in the Palm Cemetery. Courtesy Department of College Archives and Special Collections, Olin Library, Rollins College.

Some of the oldest headstones are hard to read, but each one provides some tantalizing clue to the lives of those who went before us. There are poignant memorials to children who lived just a few hours, days, or years in the early 20th century. Looking at the markers, you are struck by the fact that wives seem to outlive their husbands by many decades no matter what the race, creed, or century. Many markers in both cemeteries proudly note the deceased's service in World War II. Mary Brown is buried in Palm Cemetery, but the marker has been lost and there are no surviving city records to identify her resting place.

Palm Cemetery is tucked between the fairways of the Winter Park Golf Course, so don't be surprised to find a stray golf ball or two on the pathways.

Both cemeteries are part of the City of Winter Park's Department of Parks and Recreation. Both have plots for sale at relatively reasonable prices through the City of Winter Park. With the understanding that the residents are resting in both these locations and that their friends and relatives may be there for a quiet visit with them, you are welcome to stroll the grounds with due respect and enjoy the history that surrounds you.

Mr. and Mrs. Richmond J. Lawson photographed in 1994. Mr. Lawson passed away July 16, 1997. The couple operated the first—and for a long time the only—funeral home in West Winter Park. © Peter Schreyer

THE DINKY DOCK

The Orlando-Winter Park Railway–known as "The Dinky Line"–traveled behind Rollins College, along the edge of Lake Virginia, before it headed into Orlando. This is a postcard from the early 20th century.

The "Dinky Line" was a narrow-gauge railroad that began operating between Winter Park and downtown Orlando on July 24, 1888. The actual name of the railroad was the Orlando and Winter Park Railway, but Rollins students quickly gave the line its nickname. The train was so small that passengers sometimes climbed off and helped lift the cars back on the rails when the train jumped the tracks—which it did twice on its inaugural run. The line was also used to transport timber, which was hauled in boats to the Dinky Dock adjacent to the station. The Dinky Line was in operation until 1969, but the last few years it carried only freight. In 1956, the Rotary Club purchased the one-acre property where the Dinky Station had been located and donated it to the city. You'll find a plaque marking that date in the park. There are picnic tables and plenty of parking, and it is right on Lake Virginia. The public boat ramp at the Dinky Dock is the only one in the city. No admission charge.

Ollie Avenue intersects Fairbanks just across from the Winter Park Library: the Dinky Dock Boating Park is at the southern end of Ollie Avenue at Lake Virginia. At Park Avenue and Fairbanks, as you face Rollins College, turn left at the light, take Fairbanks to Ollie and turn right. The park is open from 8 a.m. until dusk for fishing, swimming, and boating. Boat permits are required and are available at the Winter Park Library. Public restrooms on site.

W. P. 5—The Beal-Maltbie Shell Museum,
Rollins College, Winter Park, Fla.

W. P. 7—The Walk of Fame, Roll
Winter Park, Fla.

...tories for Men. Rollins College. Winter Park, Florida

11

his word is good.
Hello: Hope are fine
guess you must be
now. How Fine an
your folks. I'll i
Deauville Dr
Orlando. I have a 4
Bath & utility R. car port
two home on 50 at
Hills. I me No

ROLLINS COLLEGE

PUGSLEY HALL FOR WOMEN AT ROLLINS COLLEGE, WINTER PARK, FLA.

WP-2 KNOWLES CHAPEL, ROLLINS COLLEGE,
WINTER PARK, FLORIDA

Rollins College

W.P. 25   ROLLINS HALL, BOYS' DORMITORY, ROLLINS COLLEGE, WINTER PARK, FLA.

This postcard was sent to New York in April, 1937

Rollins College is the oldest institution of higher education in the state of Florida, and the only one that can count a Nobel laureate among its graduates—Donald Cram (class of 1941) won the Nobel Prize in Chemistry in 1987. The 67-acre campus is less than a block from the intersection of Park and Fairbanks Avenues and its Mediterranean architecture blends easily with the early twentieth century look in nearby downtown. It has always been a four-year coeducational school, and it now includes both graduate and extension studies. It was founded by the Congregational Church, though it is now a secular institution.

The city's founders originally envisioned this site for a resort hotel and it is easy to see why: Rollins is situated on prime real estate on the edge of Lake Virginia. In the days before schools routinely had swimming pools, it hosted the state swimming finals, which were held right in the lake.

If you take a walk on campus and see the statue of a fox on the grass in front of the Mills Memorial Building, you are witnessing a Rollins tradition. It is the annual Fox Day, which means the weather is so fine that the President of the college has given everybody the day off. When students see that fox, they head for the beach.

Tours of Rollins are given Monday through Friday and on some Saturdays, but you need to give the school a week's notice. Call **407-646-2161** for more information.

WP-30 ANNIE RUSSEL THEATRE AND KNOWLES MEMORIAL CHAPEL, ROLLINS COLLEGE, WINTER PARK, FLA.

There are many postcards of the Knowles Chapel and the "Annie Russell".
This one misspells "Russell" by omitting the final "L".

W. P. 20   ROLLINS COLLEGE ON LAKE VIRGINIA BY MOONLIGHT. WINTER PARK, FLA.

Rollins at night in a postcard from a set of 16. Until recently,
Rollins was the source of most of Winter Park's "nightlife."

ROLLINS COLLEGE ATHLETICS

ollins athletes are called "Tars", and there are several explanations for this nickname. One alumnus told me it was because Rollins sat on a lake around which timber was harvested in the 19th century, and "Tars" refers to the tar or pitch that oozed onto the hands of the lumberjacks from the pine trees that were cut down. The school says—officially—that the name came into use during World War I, when the Navy stationed a small training vessel in Lake Virginia. "Tar" is a nickname for sailors.

If you are visiting, there will very likely be a sporting event of some sort on the Rollins schedule: from Men's and Women's Basketball to Baseball, Soccer, Tennis, Volleyball and Sailing.

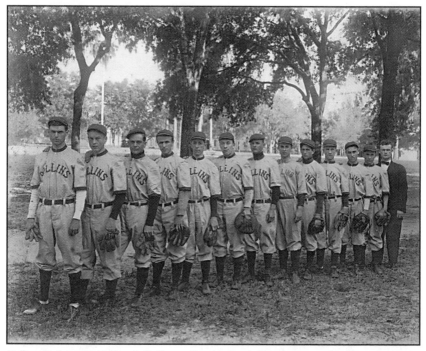

Rollins College 1912 Baseball Team. The back of the picture reads: "Mason Coach, Pratt P, Varden P, Boyer CF, Landstreet 1B, Pike C, Lee LF, Washington C, Waite 3B, Porter SS, Roberts 2B, Labree RF, Wetherell Asst. Mgr." Courtesy Department of College Archives and Special Collections, Olin Library, Rollins College.

For information on schedules call **407-646-2198**.

Horsepower at Rollins, circa 1891. Left to right: S. Waters Howe, Mamie Bidwell, Crit Coffee, Amy Allen, Kirby Smith, Burchard Kuhl, Clara Foster, A.C. Hart. Courtesy Department of College Archives and Special Collections, Olin Library, Rollins College.

Rollins students on Lake Osceola in May, 1889. Left to right, front and back: Bessie Watson, Fred Lewton, Grace Bingham, Ivy Lewton, B. Maud Coan and Wiley Abercrombie. Courtesy Department of College Archives and Special Collections, Olin Library, Rollins College.

ROLLINS COLLEGE PERFORMING ARTS

A postcard of The Annie Russell Theatre shortly after it was constructed.
Note how it appears to be sitting in the middle of a citrus grove.

Theatre and Dance   Rollins College offers a range of performances each year under the aegis of the Department of Theatre Arts and Dance (Rollins uses the British spelling of theater). Many of the performances take place in the Annie Russell Theatre, which is on the National Register of Historic Places. The "Annie Russell" is a 70-year old facility with the look and intimate feel of a Broadway theater (that's how we spell theater on Broadway). It is named after stage actress Annie Russell (1864-1936), who retired to Winter Park and took a lively interest in the college productions at Rollins. Mrs. Mary Louise Curtis Bok, a wealthy friend, donated the money to Rollins for the "Annie Russell" with the proviso that Miss Russell be allowed to serve as director of the theater during her lifetime.

Music   The Virginia S. and W.W. Nelson Department of Music schedules student performances throughout the fall, winter, and spring. Seven ensembles, four choirs, and the Rollins College Orchestra provide the college and the local area with about 50 free recitals and concerts each year. This doesn't even include the Bach Festival, and Bach Festival Concert Series, which attract nationally known artists each year to perform at Rollins.

For information on music performances call **407-646-2233**.
For more information on drama call **407-646-2145**.

BACH FESTIVAL

T he Winter Park Bach Festival began at Rollins College as a salute to Bach's birthday in 1935 and has been an annual tradition since then. Long-time Winter Park businessman and philanthropist John Tiedtke is in great part responsible for the festival's success. The fourth-oldest such festival in the United States, it has earned international recognition for the quality of its festival choir and its many guest artists. Over the years guest artists have included The Emerson String Quartet, pianist Richard Goode, and soloist Miles Hoffman. The annual festival takes place in the spring. But the Bach Festival Society now schedules concerts year-round.

Some of the concerts are in the Annie Russell Theater, on the campus of Rollins College, and some take place in the Knowles Memorial Chapel. Seating is limited so it is a good idea to buy tickets early.

Dr. John Sinclair
Conductor & Music Director

The Bach Festival Visiting Artist
&
The Bach Festival Choral Masterworks

2001-2002 CONCERT SERIES

Box Office: 407-646-2182
www.bachfestivalflorida.org

For more information on the annual festival, and the annual concert schedule, call **407-646-2182**. The festival also has a web site at **info@bachfestivalflorida.org**

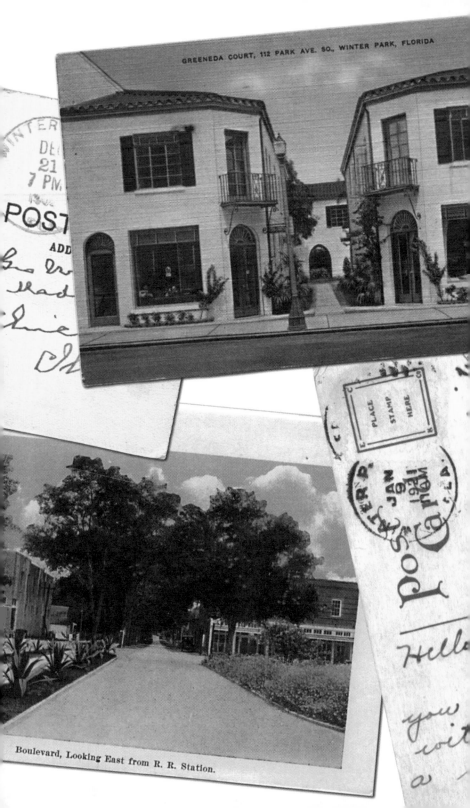

GREENEDA COURT, 112 PARK AVE. SO., WINTER PARK, FLORIDA

Boulevard, Looking East from R. R. Station.

The Avenue

Park Avenue, Business Section. Winter Park, Fla.

...dear.
...gu I wish
...were here
...me. I'm having
...nderful time
...ove Frances.

East Park Ave., Winter Park, Fla.

German made pre-1914 postcard. The porch on the building at left has since been enclosed and the building now houses Banana Republic.

A Walking Tour
STROLLING PARK AVENUE

Strolling Park Avenue is the reason most people come to Winter Park; and speaking as an experienced shopper, I must say it is an excellent one. But you could walk it for the exercise if shopping isn't your thing: the Avenue is six-tenths of a mile from Fairbanks to Swoope. If you walk up one side and down the other you can give your personal trainer the day off. Or you could walk it to learn about its history, which is evident on every block.

PARK AVENUE FROM FAIRBANKS TO NEW ENGLAND   With Rollins at your back, you begin your walk north up the Avenue; and this section has improved enormously since the city's Enhancement Project rebuilt the Avenue's streets and sidewalks (1998-2000). New businesses have moved in to mingle with the old without obliterating the 1920s character of the street. Up one block and across from City Hall is the new SunTrust Plaza. This was very controversial when it was proposed in 1996 because it included a third story and this required a variance on the Park Avenue height limitation. If you step back and look up you can see how well the new construction has been integrated into the existing building styles.

One of the few buildings that doesn't suit the Avenue at all is City Hall, built in 1962 at the corner of Park and Lyman. It is one of those 1960s buildings that makes you ask: what could they have been thinking? Still, that big oak tree mercifully obscures most of it, and the city keeps it looking nice. There is a lovely statue by Albin Polasek (1879-1965) placed out front, and though the sculpture's classical style is a bit at odds with the architecture of the building, to be fair, just about anything would be. (Come to think of it, the train station in Central Park is in this same category. You'll see it later on the stroll.)

On the east side of the street you'll find the next block filled with locally owned businesses and restaurants—gratifying to see in the age of the superstore. But even as I say that, the nationally owned Pottery Barn on the Avenue's west side deserves much credit for the way it remodeled the old Colony Theater. The theater has been on Park Avenue since 1939, and the Pottery Barn managed to completely renovate it and yet keep the exterior of the building—with its landmark marquee—virtually unchanged. On the same side of the street is a historic building which now houses the Park Plaza Hotel. The original Winter Park Company was here in 1886, and in 1922 the Hamilton Hotel was built on the site. The Park Plaza renovated it in 1977, and again during the summer of 2001, but the exterior of the building looks pretty much as it did in the 1920s.

The shops at 300-326 South Park Avenue are in buildings constructed in the teens and twenties. If you look up at the shape of 310 you won't be surprised to learn

that in 1916 it housed a garage and gas station. The building on the corner of Park and New England was constructed for the Union State Bank in 1917 and the old clock dates from that period. (Sometimes the clock runs, and sometimes it doesn't, so don't set your watch by it.)

PARK AVENUE FROM NEW ENGLAND TO MORSE   At New England, Central Park begins on the west side of the street. This park, deeded to the City of Winter Park in 1911 by Charles Hosmer Morse, has always been a vital part of city life. There is a well-manicured rose garden on its edge, just across from the Park Plaza Hotel. In the early part of the 20th century they kept alligators in a pen in the park, but in 1918 someone thought better of the idea and removed them. Nowadays—sans gators—most of the city's special events take place in Central Park. In its center is a plaque honoring Morse—the man who made this green space possible.

If you turn left (west) at New England you will find the Farmers Market and the Winter Park Historical Museum just across the railroad tracks in the old railroad freight depot. If you want to see the present Amtrak Station in Central Park, continue on the west side of the street to Morse Boulevard. It is at Morse and the railroad tracks. The less said about this building, the better.

Boulevard, Looking East from R. R. Station.

Post-1915 postcard of what is now Morse Boulevard, looking toward the corner of Morse and Park.

This postcard was sent with Christmas greetings, December 1904 and postmarked in Winter Park. The Trovillion pharmacy building (far left) seems to be in every early picture of Park Avenue. There weren't many other buildings.

Back on Park Avenue, across from Central Park, at 214-218 South Park is the Henkel Building built in 1916. Just up the street at 152 South Park is an 1884 building that used to house a grocery and feed store. 142 South Park is a big white building constructed in 1911 for the Bank of Winter Park. If you look up you'll see the friezes in the shapes of wreathes across the front and two rather nifty finials draped in garlands crowning it all off. Why don't they put interesting doo-dads like that on buildings anymore?

Not far up the block at 122 South Park is the Winter Park Land Company, a descendant of the original Winter Park Company begun by Loring Chase and Oliver Chapman in the 1880s to develop Winter Park. This building was constructed in 1917.

GREENEDA COURT, 112 PARK AVE. SO., WINTER PARK, FLORIDA

A recent stash of these old postcards of Greeneda Court was found when one of the court's tenants did some spring-cleaning. Greeneda Court was built in 1947.

At 112-118 South Park you'll find the prettiest place on Park Avenue. Greeneda Court was built in 1947 by former mayor Ray Greene (hence the name), using the design of architect James Gamble Rogers II. It looks like a miniature Mediterranean hacienda, and it makes you feel as if you could move right in. As you enter the courtyard, note the detail of the Spanish tiles going up the steps on the south side of the courtyard. Even the courtyard bricks (recently redone) have style with their herringbone pattern and their nonmortared construction. Inside the courtyard you'll find tables adjacent to a Spanish-tiled fountain where you can sit and rest for a minute.

PARK AVENUE FROM MORSE TO SWOOPE　　When you return to Park, walk north toward the corner of Morse and Park. As you cross Morse, look to the east (away from the park) into the median strip. In the center of the median is the last remaining hitching post in the city. The others were removed in 1915 when the meaning of horsepower began to change and the streets had to be widened and paved to accommodate the automobile. If you turn right here and walk down a couple of blocks you will find Lake Osceola, and the dock for The Winter Park Boat Tour.

At the northwest corner of Park and Morse you will find one of the oldest buildings on the Avenue. Built in 1882, it once had an upstairs balcony. More than half a

Vista in Mr. C. H. Morse's Private Park.

century ago it housed a drug store with a soda fountain where local residents came to pass many a warm summer afternoon with a cold ice cream soda.

As you approach Park and Lincoln, you may want to take a short detour to see the home of Charles Hosmer Morse, which is a couple of blocks away. Turn right at Lincoln and walk to Interlachen and turn left. "Osceola Lodge," built in 1886, is near the northwest corner of Lincoln and Interlachen. Morse bought the house in 1904, had it remodeled, and made this his home until his death in 1921. I think the simplicity of this structure says a great deal about Mr. Morse, who certainly had the fortune to build a far more imposing home. His granddaughter Jeanette Genius McKean also lived here with her husband, Hugh McKean (Rollins President 1951-1969) until they built their own home called "Windsong" (sometimes called the Genius Estate) on Genius Drive. A proposal to open Osceola Lodge for tours was nixed in 1993.

As you return to Park Avenue, walk up half a block and at 300 North Park, look up and you'll see that the owner has added a third story here—reportedly for a

W. P. 2—The Genius Estate, Winter Park, Fla.

ST. MARGARET-MARY CATHOLIC CHURCH

*This is a postcard of the Saint Margaret Mary mission church,
located around the corner from the present church.*

3,000 square-foot apartment. He was able to do so because the city raised the height limitations on Park Avenue for the construction of the SunTrust Plaza. At the corner of Park and Canton there is a really neat courtyard built in the fashion of Greeneda Court. The Hidden Garden was constructed at the urging of the late Eve Proctor, who deserves a lot of the credit for the way Park Avenue looks today. She was the first merchant to put out planters with flowers in them on the sidewalk. Next to the Hidden Garden, the buildings are called Little Europe (look up and you will see the name on the building). Mrs. Proctor envisioned Park Avenue as one day having the ambience of a little European village, and she had quite a lot of foresight as it turns out.

Central Park ends at North Park Avenue and Garfield. For one block there are now shops on both sides of the street. The shops on the east side stop at Saint Margaret Mary Catholic Church, which once had a beautiful mission church just around the corner. On the west side the shops continue for several more blocks. But first, on the west side, at Park and Canton, you'll see the Charles Hosmer Morse Museum of American Art. It is a striking building and an imposing one. Don't let it intimidate you from going further up the street. Just past the museum are some more shops which you won't want to miss.

If you still have some pep in your step, walk just a little further to Park and Whipple where you can see the new planters, flower gardens, and benches installed adjacent to the Winter Park Golf Course. They are a memorial to Charles Hosmer Morse who gave so much to the city. On the east side of the street, behind a hedge, there is a croquet court—not exactly a common sight these days. It was built on city property with the help of the Winter Park Croquet Club. It is open to the public but the Club asks you to stop in at the Winter Park Country Club office to make a reservation to play. There are two firm rules: the players must wear all-white attire; and there is to be absolutely no swearing! Just behind the croquet court you'll see a very large house. It is Casa Feliz, which was moved to this spot from Interlachan in August 2001. *(For more on Casa Feliz, see pages 81-82.)* Finally, have a seat on one of the new benches and rest a spell, before you turn around and head back down Park.

SCENE IN CITY PARK

SHUFFLEBOARD COURT, WINTER PARK, FLORIDA

The shuffleboard courts on Park Avenue (above) were replaced by the present City Hall building. This is an especially fine postcard from the first half of the 20th century.

"An Outdoor Sport in Florida." (below) This postcard was sent in 1935 by the Winter Park Chamber of Commerce. On the message side it reads: "IT'S TIME TO START FOR FLORIDA! Winter Park invites you...May we be of assistance?" The Chamber clearly believed that playing chess outdoors would be viewed as quite exotic up north.

THINGS TO DO

Winter Park's golf course in a 1921 postcard.

A COUNTRY CLUB WITH NO TEE TIMES

The signs say Winter Park Country Club, but this is a city course and you don't have to join the club to play. In addition to the benefits it provides local golfers, it gives the city acres of green space adjacent to Park Avenue. The nine-hole golf course has no tee times. All you do is show up, pay your greens fees, and then put your ball into a tube at the first tee. When your ball drops out, it is your turn to go. Club members can reserve tee times on Wednesday and Thursday morning from 8:45 a.m. to 10:00 a.m. The course is on land once owned by Charles Hosmer Morse and his heirs, and for years the city leased the property. In 1997, the city purchased the acreage, ensuring a green space here for years to come. The club house, built in 1914 on Interlachen Avenue, is listed in the National Register of Historic Places.

Greens fees are nominal. Membership—which is not required—is slightly higher for nonresidents than for residents: but for either it is under $1,000. The course is open all year. Call **407-623-3339** for more information.

WINTER PARK MUSEUMS

N o matter how beautifully I describe Winter Park's museums, there will be some members of your family who will refuse to be persuaded. Let them stroll Park Avenue or play the links while you partake.

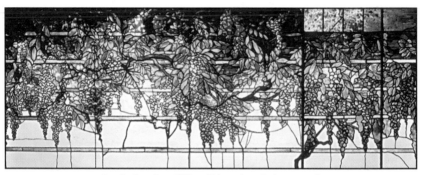

Louis Comfort Tiffany Wysteria, window panel

THE CHARLES HOSMER MORSE MUSEUM OF AMERICAN ART   This museum is a Winter Park treasure full of beauty and surprise at every turn. It houses the world's most comprehensive collection of the works of Louis Comfort Tiffany, and the museum has used that collection to create a stunning tribute to the decorative arts of the late 19th and early 20th centuries. Jeanette Genius McKean (1909-1989), granddaughter of Charles Hosmer Morse, one of Winter Park's founding fathers, began collecting Tiffany decorative items and other American art in the 1940s and 1950s. She and her husband, Hugh McKean (Rollins president 1951-1969), opened a much smaller version of the museum on the campus of Rollins College in 1942, then moved it to East Welborne Avenue. Hugh McKean had studied with Tiffany at Tiffany's home, Laurelton Hall, following his graduation from Rollins. When the neglected mansion burned in 1957, the McKeans rescued many of the home's finest windows. After Mrs. McKean's death, Mr. McKean began construction of this museum in 1995. Though he did not live to see the opening on

Louis Comfort Tiffany Peony, shade

the Fourth of July 1996, every inch of the tasteful architecture and design reflect the McKeans' sensibilities. The couple left behind an endowment so that public funds would not be required for the museum's operation. Look for the reconstructed Tiffany Chapel from the 1893 World Columbian Exposition—which was held in Chicago—and the Tiffany "Peacock Necklace," which Mrs. McKean once wore to a local party.

Louis Comfort Tiffany
Autumn, from The Four Seasons

There is a small admission charge. The museum is at the northern end of Park Avenue near the corner of Park and Canton. There is some free parking behind the museum. Open Tuesday through Saturday 9:30 a.m. to 4 p.m. and Sunday 1 p.m. to 4 p.m. Additional Friday hours September through May 4 p.m. to 8 p.m. Closed Mondays. Information available at **407-645-5311** and **407-645-5324**, and at MorseMuseum.org

WINTER PARK HISTORICAL MUSEUM   This tiny museum is maintained and operated by volunteers from the Winter Park Historical Association who are happy to answer your questions on

Winter Park history. The gift shop carries books, cards, maps, and Winter Park logo items. Exhibits rotate. It is at the north end of the Farmers Market, in the old railroad freight depot. The three-acre site is listed on the National Register of Historic Places.

Find the intersection of Park and New England and walk west (across the railroad tracks). The Historical Museum will be on your left in a red brick building. No admission charge. Open Thursdays and Fridays 11 a.m. to 3 p.m., Saturdays 9 a.m. to 1 p.m., and Sundays 1 p.m. to 4 p.m. **407-647-8180** or **407-647-2330**.

ALBIN POLASEK MUSEUM AND SCULPTURE GARDENS   Albin Polasek (pronounced Po-LASH-ek) was a Czech sculptor (1879-1965) who came to the United States in 1901 and served for thirty years as the director of the sculpture department of the Art Institute of Chicago. After World War II, the internationally known artist retired to Winter Park where he built the home and studio on Lake Osceola that now house this museum. In the summer of 2001 the beautiful gardens were expanded. The galleries were refreshed and work was done to conserve the "Emily" fountain in the front patio. The main gallery holds many of

Polasek's major works; the aviary displays several of the portrait busts he was commissioned to do during his career; and the east gallery contains works representing Polasek's Eastern European heritage. The home, the art, and the gardens tell a wonderful story of an artist and the gracious environment he created around him. The lakeside picnic tables on the estate are the best picnic spot in town.

$3 per person donation. 633 Osceola Avenue. (The museum is on that stretch of Fairbanks-Aloma-426 where the thoroughfare is briefly called Osceola). Driving to the museum from Park Avenue requires a left turn across two lanes of westbound traffic. The good news is that the worst traffic hours occur before the museum opens and after it closes. Open Tuesday-Saturday 10 a.m. to 4 p.m. and Sunday 1 p.m. to 4 p.m. Closed Mondays. It is also closed during July and August. Call **407-647-6294** for more information.

From the Cornell Museum collection: **John Frederick Kensett** *The Langdale Pike, 1958*

CORNELL FINE ARTS MUSEUM This museum on the campus of Rollins College has a collection of more than 6,000 works of art—one of the largest fine arts collections in the state of Florida. Many benefactors contributed; but it is named after George (Rollins class of 1935) and Harriet Cornell, who gave more than a million dollars to build the complex. Exhibits rotate.

*also from the
Cornell Museum collection:*

(left) **Hiram Powers**
Faith, 1867

(right) **Pietro Liberi**
*Europa crowned by Genius
c. 1640*

No admission charge. Open Tuesday through Friday 10 a.m. to 5 p.m. and Saturday and Sunday 1 p.m. to 5 p.m. Closed Mondays and major holidays. Go south on Park Avenue (crossing Fairbanks into the Rollins campus) until Park Avenue ends at Holt. Turn left (east) until Holt ends at the museum. Limited free parking available adjacent to the museum. Also at the SunTrust Parking Lot at Park and Lyman, which is just a 10-minute walk from the museum (bring your ticket for validation). More information at **407-646-2526**.

WINTER PARK'S ART FESTIVAL(S)

10th Annual Winter Park Sidewalk Art Festival
March 1976

SPRING   Park Avenue is turned over to artists and pedestrians in March every year for the Winter Park Sidewalk Art Festival. It began in 1960 and has grown from a small show, with a few exhibitors, to one of the most successful events of its kind in the country. Between 200 and 300 artists exhibit and sell their works each year, and the festival annually attracts at least 350,000 people. Artists compete in 11 different categories for thousands of dollars in prize money. *Friday, Saturday, and Sunday on the third weekend in March. For applications and other information, contact the Winter Park Sidewalk Art Festival message line at* **407-672-6390** *or log on to* **wpsaf.org**

Since the crowds can be quite large, your visit will be much more enjoyable if you plan ahead. Come early in the morning, get your car parked, get a cup of coffee, and enjoy Park Avenue before it is filled with people. March weather is usually mild, but it can be unpredictable. Bring a hat for the sun and an umbrella (just in case).

During the festival avoid coming into Winter Park on Fairbanks. Traffic on Fairbanks during festival weekend can sometimes back up from Park Avenue to I-4. Instead, take the Lee Road exit off I-4 (Exit 46) and head east on Lee. At Lee Road and

Orlando Avenue (Rt.17-92) turn right (south). Go a few blocks to Morse Boulevard and turn left (east again). Morse will take you into Winter Park. Put the car where you find a legal place!

If you miss the Festival, you can still enjoy the art. Beginning in 1969 the Festival began purchasing the Best of Show pieces each year and donating them to the city. The collection is on permanent display at the Winter Park Public Library, 460 East New England Avenue.

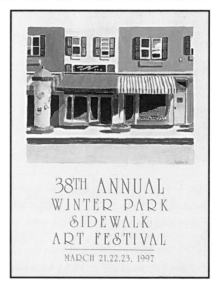

38TH ANNUAL
WINTER PARK
SIDEWALK
ART FESTIVAL
MARCH 21.22.23. 1997

AUTUMN   Because of the success of the spring festival, Winter Park has added an Autumn Art Festival. It is held on the second weekend in October each year, at Lake Island Park near the corner of Denning and Morse. For information on the autumn festival call the Winter Park Chamber of Commerce at **407-644-8281**.

Don't try this at home kids. The postcard was produced for Florida in Germany about 1900. The "little girls" appear to be dolls placed on and around stuffed alligators.

FUN FOR THE YOUNG

T he City of Winter Park, Rollins College, The Crealdé School of Art, and the Winter Park YMCA all have activities designed just for young people.

Rollins has two programs—**Talent Search** and **Upward Bound**—designed specifically for secondary students in at-risk neighborhoods. Information on those programs is available at **407-646-2282** and **646-1558**.

Rollins has a **Summer Day Camp** for children in kindergarten through the sixth grade. There are two 4-week sessions with 30 different programs to choose from. Students take part from 9:15 a.m. to 3:00 p.m., with pre-class playtimes beginning at 7:15 a.m. and post-class playtimes from 3 p.m. to 6 p.m. Information is available at the Rollins Web site: **rollins.edu** or at **407-646-2604**.

The Rollins Department of Athletics offers a **Sports Summer Camp**. Information on it can be obtained at **407-646-2366**.

The City of Winter Park has 102 parks and recreation facilities—more parks per capita than any other city in Florida. There are ongoing programs for all ages through the Parks and Recreations Department. This includes sports teams and events at the Ward Park Sports Center, as well as events, programs, and activities at the Winter Park Community Center. The city's **Cady Way Pool** is staffed and run by the Winter Park YMCA, which also runs the after-school programs at the Winter Park Community Center. Call **407-599-3334** for more information. Or stop by 151 W. Lyman, just off Park Avenue downtown, and ask for guidance. The Parks and Recreations Department has a very good map of all the city's parks and will let you know what activities are going on during your visit that might be of interest to your children.

The Winter Park YMCA has a great facility for young people called the Eastbrook YMCA Program Center. The 10-acre site has after-school programs, many field-related sports teams, a swim team and a Summer Day Camp. Call the **Winter Park YMCA** at **407-644-1509** for more information.

Both the young and the young at heart will enjoy a visit to the **Crealdé School of Art**. As a not-for-profit its fees are affordable, and though it has more classes for adults than children, its programs for kids—including its Art Camp—have brought it much acclaim. Crealdé is at 600 St. Andrews Boulevard, about three-quarters of a mile east of the intersection of Aloma of Lakemont Avenues. For more information call **407-671-1886**.

OTHER SPECIAL EVENTS

Winter Park has a number of celebrations, festivals, sales and parades along Park Avenue. As the dates of these events vary from year to year, consult the city's Calendar of Events, available at City Hall, or log on to ci.winter-park.fl.us

SPRING
St. Patrick's Day Parade
Sidewalk Art Festival
10 K Road Race
Easter Egg Hunt
Orlando Philharmonic Spring
    Concert
Run for the Trees 5K
MS Walk

SUMMER
WLOQ Jazz Concert Series
Old Fashioned 4th of July
    Celebration
City Summer Camp
Christmas in July Sale on Park

WINTER
(Christmas Events) Santa's Sleigh
Ride and Central Park Tree
Lighting; Christmas Parade;
Christmas in the Park; Window
Painting on the Avenue;
Christmas Card Competition.
Santa Visits Winter Park
    Neighborhoods
(January) Martin Luther King, Jr.,
    Celebration

FALL
Halloween Haunts Park Avenue
Autumn Art Festival
Orlando Philharmonic
    Fall Concert
"Kids for Kids" Day

FARMERS MARKET

For 22 years local residents have been stopping by the Winter Park Farmers Market on Saturday morning for fresh produce, plants, and other goodies. In fact residents rate it as the best social activity in the city. Following the expansion of the Market in 1995, the local secret is now out. Between 4,000 and 5,000 people drop in each Saturday morning to shop the stalls of 50-70 vendors. Located in and around the old brick railroad freight depot on New York Avenue, the market now has both indoor and outdoor areas as well as tables covered by sun umbrellas where you can sip your coffee and watch the hubbub. Depending on the season, you can find vine-ripened tomatoes, Vidalia onions, sweet corn, and other harvests of the South. You can always buy coffee and something to munch on—including fresh bagels, Russian pastry, knishes, and rugelach. Other recent offerings include Mountain Kettle Corn (salty and sweet) and fresh barbeque cooked on location. Come early for the best of what's available.

Even if you don't need any plants, just enjoy the beautiful display. I stopped by recently and, walking through the annuals and perennials, I caught the scent of jasmine that filled the air. *Open Saturday 7 a.m. to 1 p.m. except during the Sidewalk Art Festival. No admission charge. You can bring your dog if it is on a leash. The facility is a city park and is available for special events. Restrooms on site.*

Located on New York Avenue between New England and Lyman. New England between Park Avenue and New York is closed to automobile traffic each Saturday morning to better accommodate pedestrians. From Park Avenue walk west on New England one block. The Farmers Market will be on your left. For more information call **407-599-3329**.

ളᎾ

Sorting oranges in Winter Park at the turn of the 20th century. Courtesy Department of College Archives and Special Collections, Olin Library, Rollins College.

W. P. 3—Genius Drive, Winter Park, Fla.

The Scenic Drive, Winter Park, Florida

Rollins College from Lake Virginia.

CITY OF NEIGHBORHOODS

THE SCENIC DRIVE

A marked routing through residential sections of Winter Park, Florida. Motorists following this route pass along streets arched with aged, moss-hung oaks, around lakeshores and past magnificent homes and gardens. This view shows the Scenic Drive approaching the Kraft Memorial Azalea Gardens

Winter Park Fla. Sept. 1-1941. 76° at am 90

POST CARD

Dear Friends: I am thinking of Warren St. friends + while my eyes

Mrs Ross McKay

W. P. 12—Towering Oak Trees Line Beautiful Interlachen Avenue, Winter Park, Florida

Architect
JAMES GAMBLE ROGERS II

rchitect James Gamble Rogers II (1901-1990) had more influence on the style and quality of Winter Park's homes than perhaps any other single individual. His uncle was a prominent architect in the Northeast. His father was also an architect, who moved to Florida for his health in 1916. James Gamble Rogers II went to high school in Daytona Beach, then worked his way through Dartmouth College, where he studied engineering and architecture. In 1928 he established a branch office of his father's architecture firm in Winter Park.

His first project in Winter Park was on the Isle of Sicily, now an exclusive enclave, but then a swampy outcropping into Lake Maitland. He surveyed and reclaimed the

Rogers in his office about 1940. Note the Frank-Lloyd-Wright-ish fabric in the drapes. Photo courtesy of John H. Rogers.

land and then built a French Provincial house for himself and his wife there. It was so stunning, that the ensuing publicity launched his career.

The story goes that one day, after he had built his house on the Isle of Sicily, a couple knocked on his door and asked the name of the architect who had designed the home. When Rogers said *he* was the architect, Mr. and Mrs. Robert Barbour hired him on the spot to design a house for them. Barbour gave Rogers a budget and a free hand on the design. The home became Casa Feliz, a copy of an Andalusian farmhouse on the edge of Lake Osceola. Casa Feliz was photographed for numerous magazines and led to even more commissions for the young architect.

Rogers designed more than 50 homes in Winter Park and the surrounding areas. And though he never gave up creating beautiful homes, after World War II he turned toward designing public buildings as well. These include the The Mills Memorial Library at Rollins and the Florida Supreme Court building in Tallahassee—which got so much air time during the 2000 Presidential election.

In 1941 he and his wife sold their home on the Isle of Sicily and built a Greek revival home on 17 acres off Palmer Avenue that had once been a part of W.C. Temple's groves. The original Temple orange tree was a part of that estate.

A rare postcard of Rogers' home on Winter Park's Isle of Sicily. It was the first home built on the Isle. Most of the house has since been razed.

During his lifetime, Rogers was known as a modest, funny, and thoughtful man. Once a client asked him how he could design such excellent Spanish revival homes, since he had never been to Spain. *"Sir, I've never heard anyone argue that Leonardo da Vinci attended the Last Supper,"* he said. *"But he painted a pretty creditable picture of it."*

Rogers had two sons, John H. and James Gamble IV. John became an architect and joined the family firm, Rogers, Lovelock and Fritz, where he is now the president. James (called Jimmy when he was growing up) became a folksinger—using the name Gamble Rogers since there already was a folksinger named Jimmy Rogers. He was part of the successful Serendipity Singers in the 1960s, and later worked as a solo singer, songwriter, and storyteller. He was also a regular on National Public Radio. In 1991 he lost his life attempting to rescue a drowning swimmer in the surf at Flagler Beach, Florida. The annual Gamble Rogers Folk Festival in St. Augustine is named in his honor.

In Winter Park any resident who wants to give his home an air of quality implies that it is a James Gamble Rogers II home or that Rogers II was somehow involved in its remodel or update. If all these rumors were true it would mean James Gamble Rogers II was the architect on virtually every home in Winter Park. If you think about it, this is an amazing tribute to this talented man. If you would like to see a few of the best of his designs, turn the page and take the Driving Tour.

Charles Hosmer Morse and unidentified man standing on the porch at Osceola Lodge, about 1915.
Courtesy Department of College Archives and Special Collections, Olin Library, Rollins College.

A Driving Tour
WINTER PARK BY CAR

When you are tired of walking, you might enjoy seeing the city from your car window. This tour is about 10 miles, and in an hour and a half will take you through some of Winter Park's prettiest neighborhoods. Remember to be neighborly as you drive, and to drive with care.

Begin at **Park Avenue** and **Canton**—just before you get to Saint Margaret Mary Catholic Church. If you are pointed away from Rollins College (north) on Park, turn right (east) onto Canton and drive one block to **Knowles**. Turn right on Knowles. On your left is an apartment house on the corner, then two houses, then another apartment house, and then you will come to:

> **232 Knowles** on the left side of the street. Built in 1886, it is called **Knowles Cottage** because it was one of the first homes built by **Francis B. Knowles**, an original shareholder in The Winter Park Company. His early fortune came from making and selling gloves for the Union Army.

Continue on Knowles to **Lincoln** and turn left. Lincoln isn't a busy street, so you may be able to pull to the side of the street and park. Walk to **Interlachen** and turn left. On your left, at **231 Interlachen**, is **Osceola Lodge** built in **1882**.

Osceola Lodge was also built by **Knowles** and was enlarged in 1904 by **Charles Hosmer Morse**. It was here that Morse died in 1921. Morse was a great benefactor to the City of Winter Park, and he clearly could have lived in a much more pretentious home. Though modest, the home is on a wonderful piece of real estate. The property extends across the street down to Lake Osceola.

Once you are back in your car, turn left from Lincoln onto Interlachen. On your left at **301 Interlachen** is a house designed by **James Gamble Rogers II**. It incorporates the Creole-style ironwork you'll see on a number of his homes. When you come out of the trees you will see the **Club House** of the **Winter Park County Club** on the left side of the street near the intersection of **Old England** and Interlachen. Built in 1914, its early date as a recreation facility in Florida, and its Craftsman style, have earned it a place on the **National Register of Historic Places**. Turn left into the parking lot, and if you are so inclined, park the car and walk to the driveway of the Club House. If you stand with the Club House sign perpendicular to your right shoulder, your nose will be pointing toward some pine trees across Interlachen. High up in a tall pine tree that slants to the right, you will see a large nest. It is the nest of a bald eagle and from time to time you can spot the occupants. Eagles return year after year to the same nest. When you have returned to your car, turn left out of the parking lot onto Interlachen. At the intersection of Interlachen and **Webster** turn right. If you slow down and look to your left, you will see **Edwards House** at **461 East Webster Avenue**.

Country Club.

The Club House of the WInter Park Country Club. This postcard was produced long before the building was added to the National Register of Historic Places.

Edwards House—sometimes called Orchard Place because it was surrounded by the Henkel citrus groves—was built in **1915** by **Benjamin E. Edwards.** The home has four fireplaces, which is fairly unusual in Florida. Edwards' daughter Grace was the founder of the Winter Park Garden Club. In 1925 she loaned the club $5 so it could join the Florida Federation of Garden Clubs.

Continue on **East Webster** to **Georgia Avenue** and turn left. At **Seminole Drive,** turn right. As the road begins to curve to the left, you will see a striking red brick Tudor Revival home on your right. Next door at **646 Seminole,** you will see one of the oldest oak trees in Winter Park. It is believed to be at least 200 years old. The house is also a James Gamble Rogers II design. Continue on Seminole to **Palmer Avenue** and turn left. Look at your odometer, drive one-half of a mile, and look for **225 Palmer** on your right. Drive slowly, as this house can be obscured by a hedge and there is no place to pull over and stop.

Mizener House at **225 Palmer** was built in 1936 for Mrs. Mildred Mizener. Its architect, James Gamble Rogers II, described it as a bit of an oddity, since the owner wanted a Southern Colonial with none of the usual adornments, including shutters. Although she built a mansion, she was thrifty, he said, and didn't want to have to paint her trim every year.

The Mizener House in a postcard from the 1940s.
Mrs. Mizener did indeed spell her name with that added "e."

You could hardly miss the house next to Mizener House, constructed by a professional athlete. It is the largest home in Winter Park. Continue on Palmer as it becomes a one-way street and move into the left-hand lane. Turn left on **Park Avenue**, and then turn left again onto **Stovin Avenue**. Stovin angles back onto Palmer. Turn right onto Palmer. On your left will be the large pro-athlete's house (again), and then the Mizener house (again). Up the road a short way, slow down as you cross the little bridge with the pink flamingos painted on it. The flamingos appeared one night on the bridge, and they've been there ever since. Just past the bridge, turn left onto **Alabama Drive**. To your right are mostly contemporary homes. To your left is the canal between **Lake Osceola** and **Lake Maitland**. Those low buildings you see on the left are boathouses along the canal. As you reach Lake Maitland, the road curves to the right and the **Kraft Memorial Azalea Gardens** will be on your left. The park is a great place to view Lake Maitland— especially at sunset. When you continue on Alabama, you'll see Lake Maitland emerge again on your left. At the top of the hill, where the road curves to the right, you will see The Alabama on your right. Pull ahead to **Via Tuscany**, stop if you can, and look back at the old hotel.

The Alabama is the only old hotel in Winter Park that is still standing. Here it is seen in a postcard more than half a century old.

The **Hotel Alabama** was completed in 1922 and served guests until 1979, when it was converted into condominiums. It was built on the site of **W.C. Temple's** groves. Just beyond the Alabama, at **1700 Alabama Drive**, is **Temple House**, built in 1878. It was moved to make way for the hotel, and is now part of the Alabama complex. Carrie Temple purchased the home in 1904. Her husband was part owner of the Pittsburgh Pirates, and the Temple orange is named after him.

The actress Annie Russell lived in this home from 1926 until her
death a decade later. This postcard is undated.

If you have already turned left onto **Via Tuscany**, drive about half a block until you reach **1420 Via Tuscany**. The house is on your right, and you should pull over and stop if you can. This is the **Annie Russell House**.

English-born stage actress **Annie Russell** (1864-1936) bought this house in **1926**. During the 1926 hurricane, she seriously injured one of her legs when the wind swept away the cellar doors she was trying to close and pinned her under some debris. She was known for her work that helped to bring theater and other cultural activities to Winter Park. The **Annie Russell Theatre** at **Rollins College** is named after her.

Continue on **Via Tuscany** to **Via Lugano** and turn right. Residents call this neighborhood **"The Vias"**—for obvious reasons—and it contains some of Winter Park's priciest homes. When you reach **Temple Drive**, turn right. Ahead on your left is Lake Knowles, where residents float a lighted Christmas tree on a raft each December. At the intersection of Temple and **Via Capri**, turn right again. Via Capri was once the driveway of the house you see directly ahead at the end of Via Capri on **Via Tuscany**. It is called **Sandscove**.

Sandscove, at **1461 Via Tuscany**, was built in 1918 by James Stokes of Connecticut, who died before he could move in. This gorgeous home was once surrounded by five acres of lawn, and even more acres of citrus groves, which also lined the driveway.

At Via Capri and **Via Tuscany** turn left. Turn left again at the next street, which is **Via Salerno**. On both sides of the street, in the gardens of these homes, you'll see the remnants of Sandcove's citrus groves. When you reach **Temple Drive**, turn right. Take Temple to **Palmer** and turn left. Take Palmer to **Bonita Drive** and turn right. Now you are on another street that used to be the driveway of a grove house. For the first few blocks the homes are fairly modest. Suddenly, they bloom into mansions. That's because the shore of Lake Osceola is now on your right and many of these homes have a lake view. At the intersection of Bonita and **Elizabeth Drive** (the address is 1430 Elizabeth but the address is hard to spot) on your right is an Andalusian Revival home designed by James Gamble Rogers II in 1937. The exquisite details of this home are typical of Rogers' work before World War II. Note the interesting round "tower" room. Just ahead at 724 Bonita, on the other side of the street, you'll find one of the oldest homes in Winter Park. Pull past the house, if you can, and look back for the best view.

Eastbank, built in **1883**, was named for its location on the eastern bank of Lake Osceola. It was built by **William C. Comstock**, former president of the Chicago Board of Trade, who incorporated an 1877 farmhouse built by Wilson Phelps into the structure. (The Phelps farm is where Mary Brown and Mary McClure went frequently to drop off and pick up their mail.) Imagine this house surrounded as it once was by 60 acres of orange groves, with camphor trees lining Bonita Drive, which was its driveway, and a clear vista down to Lake Osceola. It is on the **National Register of Historic Places**. Mr. Comstock died in 1925, and since 1928 the home has been in the hands of the same Winter Park family. They have made it a point to re-acquire as much of Mr. Comstock's original furniture as possible.

The Comstock estate "Eastbank" in the 1890s. Courtesy Department of College Archives and Special Collections, Olin Library, Rollins College.

Just beyond Eastbank, you'll find **Maiden Lane** where you will turn left. At Maiden and **Bryan Avenue**, turn right. Bryan curves around and becomes Sylvan, which will take you to **Aloma Avenue**. Turn right onto Aloma. As you drive down Aloma, look for a street called **Jo-Al-Ca Avenue** on your right. Just past Jo-Al-Ca will be **Waddell House**, also on your right. You won't be able to slow down or pull over. Either turn into **Cortland Avenue**, so that you can stop and read about the house, or look quickly and move on.

The **Waddell House** at **1331 Aloma** was built in **1897** when the estate included 10 acres. You can see the tangled remains of the citrus grove surrounding the house. The property was subdivided in **1923** by Carl H. Galloway, who named the nearby street Jo-Al-Ca after his three boys: Joe, Al, and Carl.

Further down Aloma, where it becomes **Osceola**, the **Polasek Museum** will be on your right. Just beyond the museum you will see a small house surrounded by a white picket fence. It is **Ward Cottage**. If you want a better look, turn right into **Osceola Court**.

SCENE ON CANAL BETWEEN LAKES VIRGINIA AND OSCEOLA

Ward Cottage was built in 1883 by the **Reverend Charles W. Ward**, who was the city's first Episcopal minister. Out front a bronze plaque commemorates the home's use as the first women's dormitory for **Rollins College**.

Just past **Osceola Court** there is a right fork off Fairbanks that will take you to **Chase**. Exit right, then turn right onto **Chase** and then left onto **East New England**. There is parking on the street, and if you can find a spot, park your car and get out for a minute. This street was once the roadway into the **Old Seminole Hotel**, built in **1886**, which was destroyed by fire in **1902**. If you walk up New England a little

A postcard of the Congregational Church. This building was the church's second, constructed in 1924.

further, on your left you will pass the site of the old Langford Hotel, built in 1956, which closed in 2000. (In the summer of 2001, construction began for a new hotel on the site.) Many famous guests stayed at the Langford during its heyday, including Mamie Eisenhower and Bob Dylan (imagining them there at the same time is interesting, but I don't think it happened). At the intersection of New England and Interlachen look to your right for the First Congregational Church of Winter Park.

The church was established in 1885 under **Reverend Dr. Edward Hooker**, who became the first president of Rollins College. The present structure was built in **1924**. The 1885 bell from the original church is now in the **Knowles Chapel** at Rollins.

When you have returned to your car, drive back up **New England Avenue** toward Interlachen. At New England and **Interlachen** turn left. Up the street on your right is the **Woman's Club of**

The Winter Park Woman's Club in an early postcard.

Winter Park—built in 1921—and on your left is the **All Saints Episcopal Church**, both of which are on the National Register of Historic Places. At Interlachen and Fairbanks/Osceola turn right. Turn left at the Park Avenue light, and left again at **Holt** into the campus of **Rollins College**. After the second speed bump or about one-tenth of a mile, you will see a wide space of lawn on your right. In front of it are a few parking spots for visitors and if you are lucky, one of them might be empty. Park your car and walk toward the large buildings to your left as you face the lawn and you will see **Pinehurst Hall**.

Fires were a serious danger in the early part of this century and they destroyed most of the original buildings at the college. **Pinehurst**, built in 1886 as a women's dormitory, is the only original building that has survived. It has served many purposes since then and is still in use.

As you return to your car, you can walk past the **Rollins Walk of Fame** which is on the edge of the lawn. The walk honors respected men and women of achievement—not necessarily those who have visited Rollins. Across Holt, opposite the lawn, is **Knowles Chapel**, one of the most beautiful buildings at Rollins. On past the chapel, is the **Annie Russell Theatre**. Once back in your car, continue on Holt to the bottom of the hill, where you will find the **Cornell Fine Arts Museum**. Use the parking lot to turn around and head back up Holt. Pass the intersection

WP-5   THE WALK OF FAME, ROLLINS COLLEGE, WINTER PARK, FLORIDA

This card was sent to potential buyers during the Florida land boom of the 1920s. My house was built in this neighborhood in 1927, so this card predates that construction in "Florida's Finest New Sub-Division."

of Holt and Park, where there is a stop sign, then turn left at a tiny street called **Alfred J. Hanna Way** (a street that is almost shorter than its name). Turn left again onto **French Avenue**. At the bottom of the hill French curves to the right and becomes **Lakeview Drive**. As you drive around **Lake Virginia**, you are now in an old neighborhood called **"Virginia Heights."** At **1023 Lakeview** there is a dandy pink and green Victorian Revival that always attracts attention. All these homes have frontage and docks on the lake. Keep your eye out for turtles in the road. (I say this because a Florida snapping turtle, about 22 inches across, recently stopped traffic on Lakeview. Another driver and I got out and managed to get it turned around and out of the road without getting ourselves snapped at. Once on the grass it made a beeline for the lake!) At the intersection of Lakeview and **Stirling Avenue**, turn left. Drive less than a block and you will see **College Point** on your left. Turn left. At **1250 College Point**, there is yet another James Gamble Rogers II design. The home was built in 1955 and its modern lines are a change from his classic styles. As you exit College Point, which is a cul-de-sac, you will be on **Highland Road**. Take Highland less than a block to **Virginia Drive** and turn left.

Rollins College from Lake Virginia.

Postcard from the early 20th century, looking across Lake Virginia towards Rollins. Note how few buildings are visible.

Look for the homes at these addresses on **Virginia Drive**: **147**, **181**, **210**, and **247**. These four homes were built between 1925 and 1931 on land subdivided by **Dr. N. L. Bryan**, a Winter Park dentist, who lived at number 147. Former mayor **Herbert Halverstadt** (1945-1947) lived at number 181.

From **Virginia** turn right onto **Forest Avenue**. Take Forest to **Lake Sue Avenue** and turn right. Follow Lake Sue about one-half of a mile to **Fawsett Road** and turn left. Fawsett curves around the shore of **Lake Sue** close to the line between Winter Park and the City of Orlando. There are old houses here that have been redone and others that have not. There are new houses made to look like old houses and there are houses under construction. This is great real estate and the upscale homes reflect it. Enjoy the homes to your left and the lake view to your right. When you reach **Glencoe Road**, turn left. On your right at **2210 Glencoe** there is a Tudor Revival worth slowing down for. All that is missing is a thatched roof! When you reach **Chelton Circle**, turn left and keep Lake Chelton—which is really more of an ancient sinkhole than a lake—at you right shoulder. When you see Glencoe again, turn left. At **1873 Glencoe**, on the left side of the street, there is an interesting house. Note the old leaded glass windows on the second floor. Use caution as you cross **Lake Sue Avenue**—it can be busy. Then, head down

Glencoe on one of the few hills in Central Florida. The speed limit on Glencoe is 20 miles an hour. Don't go above the speed limit—not that you would—because the police carefully patrol here. Glencoe ends at Stirling. Turn left onto **Stirling** and at the stop sign turn right onto **Lakeview**. At Lakeview and **Antonette Avenue** there is a fork of two roads to your left—the street signs here are a little wonky and hard to read. Turn *left*, and take the *right* fork. On your left as you head up Antonette there is a big Cape Cod—it is another James Gamble Rogers II design. As you pass that home you are entering what is called **"The College Quarter."**

Most of the houses in **"The College Quarter"** are small cottages built in the 1920s to accommodate the growing faculty at Rollins. The neighborhood has retained much of its early-20th-century charm.

When you reach the top of the hill at Antonette and **Holt,** turn right onto Holt as your driving tour comes to an end. Take Holt to **Park** and turn left. As you cross **Fairbanks**, you will find yourself back in downtown Winter Park.

W. P. 1—Bird's-Eye View of Winter Park and Rollins College

The grounds of Casa Feliz–also known as the Barbour House–were once as beautiful as the home itself.

The Barbour House
CASA FELIZ

One of Winter Park's best-known homes is not on your driving tour because in the summer of 2001 it was in the process of migrating across town. Not common for a home: and even rarer for a home of its size.

Casa Feliz, also known as The Barbour House, was one of the first homes James Gamble Rogers II designed in Winter Park, and it was certainly one of his most ambitious. Robert Barbour, who had made a fortune in liquid laundry bluing, saw Rogers' home on the Isle of Sicily and hired him to design a home at 656 North Interlachen, on the west side of Lake Osceola. He gave Rogers a budget of $25,000—quite a lot of money in 1933, when President Franklin Delano Roosevelt was giving banks a holiday to ease the financial panic gripping the nation. Barbour told the architect how many rooms he wanted. Then he left the rest to Rogers. "An architect's dream," wrote Rogers half a century later.

Rogers created an Andalusian Cortijo, or Spanish farmhouse. The walls were solid brick, 12 inches thick. They were made of the used brick from the Orlando Armory, which had been razed in 1930. The red adobe roof tiles were found on a farm in North Florida, where the owner had hoped to use them in a housing development before the land boom went bust. They came to North Florida from

Cuba, and it is believed they came to Cuba from Spain. Rogers designed the light fixtures himself. Two lions heads flanking the front doorway were made from an impression owned by a Rollins professor of a lion's head at St. Peter's in Rome.

The house "received considerable national publicity" Rogers wrote, and though architectural commissions were scarce in the Depression, the attention the Barbour House received kept the young architect in business.

For nearly 70 years the house was home to a succession of owners. Then, in the year 2000, a new owner decided the renovations he desired would be more expensive than demolition, and prepared to tear down Casa Feliz. The public outcry that ensued led to Winter Park's first historic preservation ordinance. Much controversy surrounded all this, with some neighbors of Casa Feliz not especially keen on seeing the old house moved from its lot, across the street to city property. In the end, fund raising led by John H. Rogers, the son of James Gamble Rogers II, saved the house.

Then the even bigger project of moving the home off the lot was undertaken. At 1.5 million pounds the 70-by-100-foot home had to be inched up on jacks and eased across Interlachen to public property on the edge of the ninth fairway of the Winter Park Golf Course. It is probably something Mr. Rogers would not have imagined for his Andalusian Cortijo. But it means a historic treasure has been saved for all to see and enjoy. Casa Feliz, after all, means "house of happiness."

Postcard of Casa Feliz–The Barbour House–shortly after it was built in the 1930s.
The house was moved across Interlachan Avenue in the summer of 2001.

CG—4

If you'd have a mind at peace
A heart that cannot harden
Go find a door that opens wide
Into a lovely garden.

JUNGLE GROWTH AT THE MEAD BOTANICAL GARDE.
WINTER PARK, FLORIDA

A RIOT OF FLOWERS,
WINTER PARK, FLORIDA—91

WP-7   LAKE OSCEOLA, WIN

ECO TOURING

The Alligator Quartette Singing "Way Down Upon The Suwanee River," Florida.

These gators know that "Way Down upon the Suwanee River" is the Florida state song. Undated postcard.

You should be here, we down to the Beach yesterday, saw the Ocean It sure is swell here.

Em

CAUTION! GATOR CROSSING!

Before Rollins College had its own pool, swimmers used to have to keep a wary eye on the alligators that lived under the docks of Lake Virginia. Then alligators were hunted in Florida until they became endangered. After alligators became protected, they again became a nuisance in the canals between the lakes. According to an article in The *Orlando Sentinel* in 1976, one, nicknamed "Levi," was 14 feet long and made his home in the canal between Lake Sue and Lake Virginia. Another, nicknamed "Fang," was about 13 feet long and lived around the city's water treatment plant on Howell Branch Road. Just a few years ago, during mating season, a large gator stopped traffic on Fairbanks Avenue—until Orange County Animal Control arrived and made it clear to him that Fairbanks was for automobile traffic only!

The postmark on this Florida postcard is December 21, 1914.
It is rare to find a gator this size in Florida in the 21st century.

Turn-of-the-century hand-colored postcard.

Humans and alligators have been negotiating the territory around these lakes for a long time. Old timers say you used to see 15 or 20 gators each August on Winter Park's chain of lakes. In *Tales of Winter Park* Jean Shannon tells a story—which may be apocryphal—about Mr. and Mrs. Dale, the caretakers on the Comstock estate, who decided to row across Lake Osceola to church one Sunday long ago. In the middle of the lake they heard a sound, and the boat they were rowing rose out of the water. They sat quietly, hoping the boat wouldn't turn over, until the alligator beneath them settled back into the water, and they could resume their journey.

Though the population of alligators in the state is now quite large, they are increasingly rare in populated areas such as Winter Park. When they are found on golf courses and in lakes, they are usually docile, but can be dangerous if teased or surprised. But since they can be from 6 to 14 feet long and have those big teeth: if you happen to see one, you definitely wouldn't tease one, would you?

SUBTROPICAL SPECIES

Beautiful and exotic flora and fauna abound in Winter Park's subtropical environment. The alligator is the largest, but there are lots of other interesting things to see.

BALD EAGLE: The bald eagle population has grown in Florida since the species became officially protected and since the ban of DDT. Several have been known to nest in the pine and oak trees on the shores of Winter Park's lakes. There is one specific nest you can see: find the Club House of the Winter Park Golf Course at Interlachen and Webster, and stand in the driveway of the Club House with the Club House sign perpendicular to your right shoulder. Your head should be pointed to a tall pine tree across Interlachen leaning slightly southward. In the tree you will see a large nest. It is an eagle's nest, and from time to time you can spot the occupants. Eagles build these nests and then return to them year after year. With each repair and remodel the nests get bigger and bigger. You are more likely to see a bald eagle in the winter, since the heat of Florida's summer drives them north.

EASTERN GRAY SQUIRREL: Since they love oak trees, these little creatures proliferate in Winter Park. They are about 19 inches long with gray coats and tawny brown sides. They make a sort of chattering sound, especially when they think a cat or a bird is too close for comfort. They were once so prolific that they became a real nuisance in the United States, with some states offering bounties on them and others requiring landowners to turn in a certain number of squirrel pelts each season. In 1903 there were so many of them in Winter Park that the city issued special five-day squirrel-hunting licenses. But don't worry about the little creatures. That is not likely to happen again any time soon.

GREAT EGRET: The great egret is a species of wading bird that stands at least 3 feet high, is completely white, and has very long legs. Their white plumage was so coveted for women's hats that they were almost hunted into extinction. Protection brought about an increase in their population. And now many of them are so accustomed to people that it isn't unusual to see one strolling down the sidewalk along Park Avenue.

ANHINGA: This black diving bird lacks oil glands to waterproof its wings, so it can be seen sitting on docks in Winter Park, holding its wings out to dry. It is also called a snakebird for its habit of swimming with just its head and neck showing.

GREAT BLUE HERON: This is a wading bird with blue-gray wings and back. It stands about 4 feet high and has great long legs. It is a chronic loner, tolerating another heron only during mating season. Birdwatchers say many of them in Florida have lost their fear of humans. My neighborhood shares a dock on Lake Virginia, and a great blue heron does a lot of his fishing there. He hasn't heard about herons losing their fear of humans and flies away like some big prehistoric creature if you come too close.

OSPREY: This is the common name of the cosmopolitan hawk, the only bird of prey that catches its dinner in its claws instead of its beak. Its distinctive brown-and-white patterned feathers make this bird easy to spot as it soars in the thermals above Winter Park's lakes.

SLASH PINE: You will see these pines all around Winter Park, since they thrive in sandy soil. They are often very tall—some are 130 feet in height—with most of the branches up and around the top the tree.

LIVE AND WATER OAKS: Hundreds of water oaks were planted by the original developers of Winter Park, and since these trees generally live less than a century, they are continually being replaced. The live oaks are native and can live for centuries.

CABBAGE PALMETTO: These palms are native to Florida's hammock, and grow in and around wet swampy areas. The leaf bud at the treetop is a delicacy called heart of palm. This is the Florida state tree.

"We have a small cottage at Winter Park on the bank of Lake Osceola, just about the locality where the old Indian Chief Osceola had his camping ground. Occasionally we see a large alligator, but I have not yet ventured to take a ride on one of them." William A. Guild 1885

Paintings of Bald Eagle, Egret, Blue Heron, Osprey and Squirrel by Walter Ferguson © Hammond World Atlas Corp.

Politically Incorrect
SQUIRREL À LA MODE

peaking of squirrels, I found these two recipes in a 35-year-old Florida cookbook given to me by my Aunt Helen. I thought to myself, gee, what if the City of Winter Park were to reissue those five-day squirrel-hunting licenses? Would people be prepared? Both recipes are from the Florida Department of Agriculture (send any complaints to them). I present them here for fun and assume if you try them you will substitute chicken, rabbit, or some other meat for the main ingredient. If not—thanks for not sharing this information with me!

SQUIRREL PIE
Temperature: 350°F   Cooking time: 1¾ hours

1 squirrel	1 teaspoon pepper
3 tablespoons flour	½ cup fresh cut mushrooms
½ tablespoon minced parsley	2 cups stock or milk
Biscuits from mix or as below:	
2 cups flour	¼ cup fat
4 teaspoon baking powder	⅔ cup milk
½ teaspoon salt	

Disjoint and cut squirrel into 2 or 3 pieces. Cover with water and cook for one hour. Remove meat from bones in large pieces. Add flour, parsley, salt, pepper and mushrooms to the stock. Cook until it thickens (5 to 10 minutes). Add the meat and mix well. Pour into baking dish.

Make biscuits by sifting the flour, baking powder and salt together. Cut in the fat and add the milk. Stir until all dry ingredients are moistened. Roll only enough to make it fit the baking dish. Place the dough on meat in baking dish. Bake in moderate oven (350°F) until the dough is golden brown (30-40 minutes).

FRICASSEED SQUIRREL
Temperature: Low heat   Cooking time: 3½ hours

1 squirrel	3 slices bacon
½ teaspoon salt	1 tablespoon sliced onion
⅓ teaspoon pepper	1½ teaspoon lemon juice
½ cup flour	⅓ cup broth

Disjoint and cut squirrel into 6 or 7 pieces. Rub pieces with salt and pepper. Roll in flour. Pan fry with chopped bacon for 30 minutes. Add onion, lemon juice, broth, and cover tightly. Cook slowly for 3 hours.

Variation: Add 1 tablespoon paprika, ½ teaspoon cayenne, 1 sliced sour apple, and 2 cups broth instead of bacon, and lemon juice called for above.

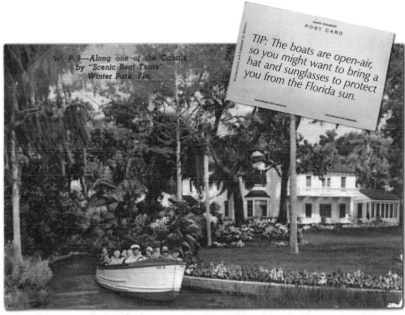

Postmarked January 1954, in Auburndale, Florida.

WINTER PARK BY BOAT

When you are driving into Winter Park or strolling Park Avenue, it is very difficult to tell that Winter Park is set on a beautiful chain of lakes. One of the best ways to get your bearings is to take the Scenic Boat Tour, which has been a Winter Park fixture for more than 60 years.

The Scenic Boat Tour was inaugurated in 1938 by Captain Walt Meloon of the Pinecastle Boat Company. Modern-day skippers on the boats are well-versed in Winter Park history and will tell you quite a lot about it as you tour the lakes—including how the lakes were instrumental in the development of Winter Park's early timber industry. You'll get a lake's-eye view of some the city's most beautiful homes. And it is a great way to see many of the different species of birds that populate Central Florida's subtropical environment.

The excursion boats leave from the dock at the foot of Morse Boulevard. From Park Avenue walk to Morse and walk east on Morse until it ends at Lake Osceola. This is just a few minutes walk from the Avenue. The boats leave every hour on the hour from 10 a.m. to 4 p.m. Open every day except Christmas Day. There is an admission charge. Information is available at **407-644-4056** and **scenicboattours.com**

Winter Park, Fla. Lake Oceola.

BOATING

There are other ways you can get out on the water in this city of lakes. Most of the lakefront docks are private, but there are these possibilities to consider:

DINKY DOCK BOATING PARK The Dinky Dock has a public boat ramp as well as parking, picnic tables, and restrooms. Boat permits are required. You can get one at the Winter Park Library just across Fairbanks from the park, or in the Finance Department at City Hall, 401 Park Avenue South. The Dinky Dock is on Lake Virginia at Ollie Avenue.

FLEET PEEPLES PARK AT LAKE BALDWIN Fleetwood Peoples (1898-1993) was the legendary swimming coach at Rollins

College who spent his retirement years teaching children to swim. And since he lived to age 95, his retirement years were long indeed. Which is why so many people in Winter Park today learned to swim from Fleet Peeples. This 23-acre park dedicated to his memory on Lake Baldwin, not far from the Pineywood Cemetery, is designed for swimming and jet skis. The boat ramp is for boats with motors under 10 horsepower. *Take Park Avenue to Fairbanks and as you face Rollins College, turn left (east) onto Fairbanks. Take Fairbanks/Aloma to Lakemont Avenue and turn right. Take Lakemont past the hospital and past the intersection with Glenridge Road. The park will be on your left. Open dawn till dusk.*

CANOES AT THE SCENIC BOAT TOUR   At the foot of Morse Boulevard, where the Scenic Boat Tour heads out into Lake Osceola each hour, there are a few canoes and rowboats available for rent. You don't need a permit to use one, and the price is just a few dollars an hour. Mornings and late afternoons are the times to see the lake at its best. The Scenic Boat Tour is open from 10 a.m. to 4 p.m. every day except Christmas.

A Sunday School outing at Lake Mizell 1890s. Courtesy Department of College Archives and Special Collections, Olin Library, Rollins College.

GARDENS

Kraft Azalea Gardens, Winter Park, Florida   5

KRAFT AZALEA GARDENS   The George Kraft Memorial Azalea Gardens are discovered by only a few of the most discerning visitors to Winter Park. Kraft himself donated the land for the 11-acre park, and in 1937 his widow provided money so the city and the Winter Park Garden Club could do the landscaping. Located in a residential neighborhood on Alabama Drive off Palmer Avenue, the gardens contain thousands of azaleas, tropical shrubs, and trees, growing along the shores of Lake Maitland. Most spectacular from January through March when the azaleas are in bloom. The Park closes at dusk. Call **407-599-3334** for more information. There are picnic tables and grills. Fishing is permitted.

Drive North on Park Avenue to Webster and turn right. Take Webster to Georgia and turn left. Take Georgia to Palmer and turn right. Take Palmer to Alabama and turn left. Gardens will be on your left. If you don't want to get out of the car, continue on Alabama and it will re-intersect Palmer. Turn right on Palmer to return to Park Avenue.

MEAD GARDEN   Mead Garden is a 55-acre botanical garden opened in 1940 in honor of Dr. Theodore L. Meade (1852-1936). Meade was a Central Florida horticulturist who studied tropical and subtropical plants and who also collected exotic orchids. The garden has picnic tables, grills, and miles of trails. Open sunrise to sunset, seven days a week. Call **407-599-3334** for more information. Restrooms on site.

Take Park Avenue south to Fairbanks and turn right at the light. Take Fairbanks to Orlando Avenue (Rt.17-92) and turn left. Just after you cross the railroad tracks, Orlando Avenue intersects Garden Drive (on the right-hand side of the road there is a brown park sign that points the way.) Turn left on Garden to the entrance.

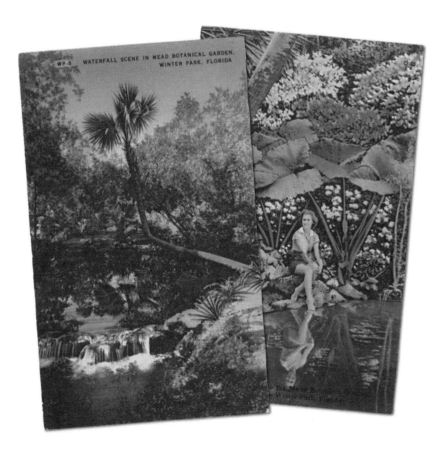

ALABAMA DRIVE, LAKE MAITLAND

SPANISH MOSS

Spanish moss (Tillandsia usneoides) is oddly enough a member of the pineapple family. Not a true moss at all, it is an epiphyte, which means it draws food and moisture directly from the air. Thus, it uses trees for support, not for nutrients. It can be seen hanging from the thousands of oak trees in Winter Park. These days it has very little commercial use. But 200 years ago Southern settlers fed it to their cattle. During the Civil War the South developed another use for it. There was almost no wool production in the South, and the shipping blockade during the War Between the States made the supply of imported wool unreliable. The Confederates cured the moss, stripped off its silver coating, and wove it into horse blankets for the cavalry.

When citrus groves were planted in Florida after the Civil War, Spanish moss was used as packing material to keep the oranges from getting bruised during shipping to the North. Then, in the early 20th century, the moss was used as a filling for furniture cushions and automobile seats.

Polly Hotard, the wife of one of Winter Park's early doctors, says in *Tales of Winter Park* that she and her friends once dressed up as "moss fairies" for the annual Osceola Day celebration. Their costumes were made of Spanish moss that they draped all over themselves. What they didn't know, but learned that day, was that Spanish moss can be full of chiggers. She says they itched for weeks.

I sometimes use Spanish moss to fill in around the base of an indoor orchid. But I too have learned about the bugs, and always spray it carefully and let it dry before bringing it into the house.

HURRICANES

Florida is in the subtropics and hurricanes are a fact of life. The hurricane season stretches from June 1 to November 30 each year. Hurricanes were not given names until 1953; consequently, all the storms before that date are designated by a year and a letter of the phonetic alphabet. For example: "1926 Able", for the first hurricane of that season, "1926 Baker", for the second, and so on.

Hurricanes hit Central Florida in 1880, 1894, and 1898, but the population was so small that damage was limited. That changed in the 20th century. The 1926 July hurricane did significant damage to Winter Park. It uprooted large oak and pines trees and wiped out the city's electrical and telephone systems. A hurricane in 1928 killed 2,500 people in Belle Glade and Pahoke, but Winter Park escaped its direct path. The 1944 October hurricane caused heavy damage in Winter Park. Classes were cancelled at Rollins, and because there was no electricity in the city, residents were required to abide by a curfew. In 1960, Hurricane Donna hit the state and it did quite a bit of damage to Winter Park. It brought heavy rains and caused considerable flooding.

In September 1999, Hurricane Floyd—one of the largest storms in modern history—loomed off the Atlantic Coast and appeared to be heading in a direct path for Central Florida. For the first time in its history, Walt Disney World® closed its doors for a day and a half. As Winter Park prepared for the worst, Floyd turned north and Central Florida was spared. The day the storm had been expected there wasn't a cloud in the sky—nor a person stirring on Park Avenue. All the shops were boarded up tight.

Today satellites can track a storm's movement and allow meteorologists to give warning of its path. If you visit during hurricane season, just make sure you keep yourself posted daily on the weather outlook.

The 1944 hurricane did considerable damage to Winter Park. Someone made these postcards of the aftermath. Courtesy Department of College Archives and Special Collections, Olin Library, Rollins College.

This is a postcard (at left) of what is now Morse Boulevard. Note the early electric light dangling across the street. These used to be taken down and stored during the summer months.

HIGH SCHOOL, WINTER PARK, FLA.

THE BOULEVARD, WINTER PARK, FLA.

105477

Postcard of Winter Park High School in 1929 (above). When did you last send a postcard to someone of your high school?

The Beal-Maltbie Shell Museum (below) was a feature at Rollins College from 1941 though 1988, when the collection was donated to the University of Florida. This postcard shows why the museum was such a hit with kids.

NT CLAM SHELL, BEAL-MALTBIE SHELL MUSEUM, ROLLINS COLLEGE, WINTER PARK, FLORIDA

WINTER PARK VILLAGE

Winter Park Village is a new shopping center one mile west of Park Avenue on Orlando Avenue (Rt.17-92) between Canton and Webster. It is on the site of the old Winter Park Mall—and is it ever an improvement! The "Village" has been an immediate success. It brought a new movie complex to the city and a number of new retail outlets and eateries. In fact, it has been so successful, that it is sometimes challenging to find parking there on a weekend evening. This is the kind of problem businesses dream of, and it doesn't seem to have, in any way, reduced the size of the throngs filling the "Village." I find the layout just a tad awkward, but the shops and restaurants are great and there is much to see and do.

Winter Park Mall Shopping Center, Winter Park, Florida

Winter Park Village replaced the old Winter Park Mall, (seen in the postcard above) one of Central Florida's first malls.

I LOVE THE NIGHTLIFE

Just a few years ago the three words "Winter Park Nightlife" would have drawn a chuckle or two. There wasn't much going on in and around the city after 7 p.m. that was not for: (a) Rollins students; or (b) people over seventy years of age. Not that there is anything wrong with either of those categories: there just wasn't much for anyone else.

In January of 2000, the City of Winter Park began easing up on what are called "café ordinances," that had not allowed restaurants to set tables on the sidewalk and had not allowed patrons to be served liquor at open-air tables. In July of 2000 they eased the ordinances a bit more. Voila! This change in the law has transformed Winter Park at night. Winter Park Village has become a real hot spot at night with its movie complex and its own "avenue" and restaurants. In fact, the popularity of the Village may have caused Park Avenue to stay open later too. Evening weather in the summer is in the 70s (20°C) and evening weather in the winter rarely requires more than a sweater. A table at a sidewalk café in Winter Park on a mild evening is now a very interesting place to watch the world go by.

Look for the spelling "goofs" in these old postcards.

The Challenge of Winter Park Spelling
THE NAME GAME

The spelling of names and street names in Winter Park is what you might call variable. Let's look at a few examples:

WELBORNE AVENUE: This avenue was named after Judge J.F. Welborne, who came to Winter Park in the early 1880s and was involved in the drafting of its early charter. Considering the trouble his name has given us, I personally wish he'd been born a Smith. All of the street signs identify this avenue as Welborne. But businesses on the street have traditionally identified their addresses as being on *Welbourne*. I went back to the old literature to find out how the judge spelled his name and found these variations in the early documents (sometimes on the same page): Welborne, Welbourne, Welborn, and (in Blackman's History of Orange County, 1927) Wellborne. I'd say you be the judge, but then you would think I was trying to be funny.

MIZENER HOUSE: This home on Palmer was built by Mrs. Mildred Mizener in 1936. Because there are some famous *Mizners* (sans one "e") in South Florida, some people spell the name of the house on Palmer with only one "e" as well. But in Mildred's obituary—which one can only hope was correct—it was spelled Mizener, and this is also how her name was spelled in the documents of her architect.

IRVING BACHELLER: This is the name of a writer who had a house on Park Avenue North. He was very famous in his day—his novel *Eben Holden* was a best seller in 1900—and Winter Park was duly proud of him. He is largely forgotten now (raise your hand if you've read *Eben Holden*) and worse yet many of us have forgotten how he spells his name. It is sometimes spelled Batcheller, or Batchelor, probably because there were some early residents with names spelled in those ways. But his entry in Who's Who spells it Bacheller and that is correct.

PINEYWOODS CEMETERY: This is how the city spells it today. But in early reference work I found it called Piney Woods, Pinewood, and Pineywood.

WOMAN'S CLUB: It is often written as Women's Club, but Woman's Club is correct.

MARY BROWN: I think everybody agrees her name was Brown. But just so you won't feel as if you are the only person with spelling challenges, in one copy of her will, *written by her own lawyer*, her name is spelled Browne. Presumably her lawyer dozed off here because all the other versions of her will spell her name without the "e".

This is the 19th century home of Judge Welborne (or Welbourne, or Wellborne or Welborn). He is remembered as the man who helped Winter Park draw up its town charter. Unfortunately the memory of how he spelled his name is not quite as clear. Courtesy Department of College Archives and Special Collections, Olin Library, Rollins College.

PICKING ORANGES IN WINTER PARK, FLORIDA

Winter Park has long ago said farewell to its citrus industry, but it lives on in this old postcard and others like it, which are now avidly collected.

"Summer heat and everyone—nearly—wearing white, birds singing, flowers fragrant, fruit plentiful. All good." Postcard from "Jessica" visiting Winter Park, to "Mrs. O. S.A." of Sandusky, Ohio, March 1932

SAYING FAREWELL

It is hard for a city to hang on to its character. American cities—and many cities all over the world—have been homogenized by the needs of modern citizens in a modern environment. In the midst of this, something very fortuitous has happened in Winter Park. It has been able to move into the 21st century with prosperity and foresight without losing the early-20th century qualities that make it unique. It is a working, thriving city, not a stage set designed just for visitors. Within its boundaries are modern businesses, modern industry, all sorts of neighborhoods, and many century-old features adapted to 21st century use. As it did long ago, Winter Park still welcomes visitors who marvel at its winter sunshine, its summer thunderstorms, its beautiful gardens, and its exotic appeal. It is a great place to visit. And it is an even better place to live. So don't say goodbye: say farewell instead. Because you just never know when you might come back. To stay.

"The weather fine. Sitting on porch in shirt sleeves. They have sweet pears here 10 feet high." Postcard from "Frank and Edith" in Winter Park, to "Mrs. E. F. B.," Chatham, New Jersey, March 1933

"This is a very pretty city and we like it. No chance for ice racing, but plenty of places to fish." Postcard from "L.M." in Winter Park, to "Mr. C.P.D.," Derry, New Hampshire, January 1946

"Such a wonderful change. Am sitting under the bluest sky in the shade of orange and grapefruit trees perfectly comfortable in a thin dress at 5 p.m. Mmmmmm!!" Postcard from "P.B.D." in Winter Park, to "Mrs. L.E.," Worcester, Massachusetts, December 1944

"This is a beautiful place the orange trees look so nice oranges lay around under the trees just like apples!" Postcard from "May" in Winter Park, to "M.E.A.," Woodland, Michigan, February 1913

BUSINESS DIRECTORY

This book would not have been possible without the support of the following businesses. If you enjoyed it, be sure to let them know.

BARRON HALL A SMALL HOME-LIKE INN, WINTER PARK, FLORIDA

ACCOMMODATIONS

The Best Western Mt Vernon Inn **407-647-1166**
Rick Frazee **800-992-3379**
110 South Orlando Avenue **bestwestern.com/mtvernoninn**
Winter Park 32789 **bwmvi@sundial.net**

The newest luxury rooms at the longest continually operated hotel in Central Florida. The only AAA Three Diamond, Mobil Three Star hotel in the City of Winter Park. The Coach Dining Room; swimming pool; nightly entertainment in the Red Fox Lounge; and the friendliest staff. Just eight-tenths of a mile from Park Avenue, and two blocks from Winter Park Village. Ask owner Rick Frazee to see his collection of more than eight hundred postcards of Winter Park.

Holiday Inn Select **407-275-9000**
Orlando East-UCF Area **hiucf.com**
12125 High Tech Avenue **sales@hiucf.com**
Orlando 32817

Renowned for its wedding and banquet facilities, this high-caliber corporate hotel features full meeting and conference facilities for 400 people. The Executive Edition provides everything a VIP guest would want, right down to the terry cloth robe.

Hampton Inn & Suites **407-282-0029**
Orlando/UCF Area   **hiucf.com**
3450 Quadrangle Boulevard   **sales@hiucf.com**
Orlando 32828

Beautiful new hotel, conveniently located off University Boulevard—adjacent to the University of Central Florida—that features an extensive complimentary Continental breakfast every morning, an outdoor heated pool, hot tub, exercise room, and gift shop. Kids stay free!

Park Plaza Hotel **407-647-1072**
Sandra "Cissie" Spang   **800-228-7220**
307 Park Avenue South   **parkplazahotel.com**
Winter Park 32789   **pkpho@mpinet.net**

This lovely, Mobil Three Star hotel is the only hotel located right on Park Avenue. Within walking distance of all Winter Park's attractions, you'll love the old fashioned service — bed turndowns, complimentary Continental breakfast in bed or on your balcony, valet service, and a great concierge. The recipient of the Winter Park Beautification Award for its balcony; it is no surprise the Park Plaza's been voted "most romantic hotel" and "best local getaway".

Thurston House **407-539-1911**
Carole Ballard   **800-843-2721**
851 Lake Avenue   **thurstonbb@aol.com**
Maitland 32751

"North Orlando's finest Bed and Breakfast." Just a short drive from many fine restaurants, Park Avenue, and Winter Park Village. The home was a winter getaway for wealthy businessman Cyrus B. Thurston of Minneapolis in the 19th century. Set amidst six lush lakefront acres, this Queen Anne Victorian will accommodate all your needs. For business travel as well as for pleasure, Thurston House is sure to please.

ACCOUNTING

Scearce, Satcher & Jung, P.A. **407-647-6441**
Kenneth L. Scearce, C.P.A. & David A. Satcher, C.P.A.   **kscearce@ssjpa.com**
243 West Park Avenue, Suite 200   **dsatcher@ssjpa.com**
Winter Park 32789

Founded January 1, 1960 by Donald L. Jung who acquired many of his clients from Lynn Pflug, Mayor of Winter Park (1958-1961), S.S.&J. offers personal service in auditing, tax, and general accounting, along with advisory services in management and business. Centrally located just across West New England from the Farmers Market. In the lobby, you'll find a fifty-five-year-old Monroe comptometer. It is the only "antique" in this progressive firm.

Thomas, Beck, Zurcher & White, P.A.
Certified Public Accountants 407-599-5900
1302 Orange Avenue
Winter Park 32789

The firm offers a wide range of accounting services including, but not limited to;
audited financial statements, tax planning and related tax preparation, pension admin-
istration, financial planning, bookkeeping services, estate planning, and technical
computer hardware and software support. Thomas A. Thomas, C.P.A., founded the firm
in August 1981. Other principals are, Gerard A. Beck, C.P.A., Carol E. Zurcher, C.P.A.,
Gregory M. White, C.P.A., and Kim C. Daniels.

ANTIQUE JEWELRY
AND ESTATE COLLECTIBLES

The Antique Buff 407-628-2111
John Buffa & Henry Friedman
334 Park Avenue North
Winter Park 32789

Offering the largest selection of unique antique and estate jewelry in Winter Park. With
a collection that dates from the early Victorian era through the 1950s, this fabulous
shop has rings, necklaces, bracelets and lockets. Also an extraordinary collection of
cameos, mourning jewelry, cuff links, stickpins, flasks, cigarette cases, men's and ladies'
wristwatches, pocket watches, fobs and chains, walking sticks, antique silver and crystal,
and sterling silver souvenir spoons.

ARCHITECTURE

Rogers, Lovelock & Fritz, Inc. 407-647-1039
John H. Rogers, A.I.A.
145 Lincoln Avenue
Winter Park 32789

Architecture, engineering, and interior design. The firm was founded in 1935 by James
Gamble Rogers II, who designed more than 50 local homes as well as a number of
well-known public and private buildings in the state. His son, John H. "Jack" Rogers,
who took the lead in saving "Casa Feliz," is president.

ART GALLERIES

Florida Frame House Art Gallery **407-644-1323**
Baxter Mathews
411 West New England Avenue
Winter Park 32789

This gallery has been a part of the Winter Park scene since 1955, which means the owner has long-term relationships with some of Florida's most gifted artists. Prints, oils, watercolors and quality framing under one roof. You'll find it in a charming bungalow one block west of the Farmers Market.

Timothy's Gallery **407-629-0707**
Carolyn Luce   **Carolyn@timothysgallery.com**
212 Park Avenue North
Winter Park 32789

Annually voted a "Top 100 Gallery of American Craft" since 1997, this gallery is a local favorite. It has one of Central Florida's most extensive collections of artistic jewelry and fine contemporary crafts. Featuring the work of both local and nationally-known artists, it has an impressive array: from whimsical doodads, to dramatically unique one-of-a-kind pieces. With blown glass, art furniture, functional ceramics, woven wearables and more, Timothy's Gallery is like a year-round art festival. Open daily.

ART STUDIES

Crealdé School of Art **407-671-1886**
Peter Schreyer, Executive Director   **crealde.org**
600 Saint Andrews Boulevard
Winter Park 32792

Located just beyond Winter Park's shopping and dining district, this school is an oasis of cultural opportunity. A not-for-profit founded in 1975, it offers more than 70 visual arts classes for adults and children. Free, changing fine arts exhibitions at The Alice and William Jenkins Gallery. Free educational exhibitions for children and adults in The Community Gallery, and one of the largest contemporary sculpture gardens in Florida. Picnic areas available along with a self-guided walking tour of the art on the grounds.

ATTORNEYS

Choosing a lawyer is an important decision that should not be based solely upon advertising.

Goldsmith, Grout & Lewis, P.A. 407-740-0144

Karen L. Goldsmith ggllaw.lawoffice.com
P.O. Box 2011 klgoldsmith@cfl.rr.com
Winter Park 32790

This is a boutique law firm, emphasizing small business administrative matters, wills, guardianships, and other personal matters. The firm prides itself in making its clients into friends by its service and concern. Please contact Goldsmith, Grout & Lewis if you would like more information on the firm.

Erik C. Larsen, P.A. 407-647-2011
Attorney and Counsellor At Law elarsen@cfl.rr.com

243 West Park Avenue, Suite 201
Winter Park 32789

Specializing in commercial transactions and real estate, Erik has maintained his office in Winter Park since 1983. He offers personalized, experienced representation in start-up ventures, as well as acquisition and disposition of real estate and other commercial assets.

Winderweedle, Haines, Ward & Woodman, P.A. 407-423-4246

250 Park Avenue South
Bank of America Building
Winter Park 32789

The law firm traces its history back to 1931 and is a full service law firm with offices in Winter Park and Orlando, serving businesses, individuals and institutions throughout Florida and the Southeast. The firm is engaged in the general practice of law, with an emphasis on general banking, real estate, corporate, commercial and municipal law, litigation, and estate planning and administration.

ATTRACTIONS

The Scenic Boat Tour 407-644-4056

Ron Hightower
312 East Morse Boulevard
Winter Park 32789

This unique attraction has been in operation since 1938, and it's a great way to see the beauty of Winter Park in a peaceful 50-minute boat ride. Open from 10 a.m. to 4 p.m., with boats departing every hour on the hour, every day except Christmas Day. Available for charters. Canoes and rowboats for rent.

Organized Jungle, Inc. **407-599-9880**
Sue Davidson   **ojinc@aol.com**
823 N. Pennsylvania Avenue
Winter Park 32789

Flowers and plants are for sale here: but this place is so much fun it definitely qualifies as an "attraction." From the sign over the door that welcomes you to "A Strange Sort of Greenhouse Place", you enter a mysterious world of rare bromeliads, exotic orchids, pots from Italy, and real nesting birds. There is a gift shop, a florist shop, a trade show department, and a business that handles interior plants. Don't miss their annual Christmas shop: it is a wow!

BANKING

Washington Mutual Bank **407-645-2492**
Linda Howard: Home Loans
Wendy Michaels: Financial Center Manager
301 South New York Avenue
Winter Park 32789

This financial services company has a history that goes back more than a century, and is now the eighth-largest banking company in the nation. With that kind of expertise, it is their mission to provide exceptional customer service along with a select array of financial products. The range includes consumer and mortgage loans and features like free checking. Now is the best time to "Join The Club" and let "Personal Banking Services" make a fan out of you!

BEAUTY

Gary Lambert Salon **407-628-8659**
Gary Lambert
517 Park Avenue South
Winter Park 32789

Gary's slogan is "Experience the Passion" and that is exactly the way he approaches each and every client. For years he has been the stylist behind many of Central Florida's best-known women. And whether you stop by for cut, color, perm or a quick shampoo and blow-dry, you'll enjoy this salon's personal attention to your needs.

Signature Strawberry Salon **407-644-6534**
& Clinical Day Spa
Debra Fisher
480 N. Orlando Avenue, Suite 112–Winter Park Village
Winter Park 32789

This is the place to be pampered with products and services that incorporate the wisdom of the East and the science of the West. Here you'll find the beautiful basics from glamorous cut and color, to special spa features such as The Sinkhole Mud Puddle Pedicure and The Sedona Strawberry Wrap that soothe and delight as they beautify. Doctor on staff for Botox and collagen injections.

BOOKS

Brandywine Books **407-644-1711**
Evelyn W. Pettit   **brandywinebooks.com**
114 Park Avenue South   **brandywine@floridabooksellers.com**
In Greeneda Court
Winter Park 32789

This wonderful little bookstore, tucked away in Greeneda Court, looks like something out of the past. In fact, it specializes in antiquarian (old) books and has a nice section on Florida. But don't let the look of the bookshop fool you. The owner, a former editor who lives thoroughly in the 21st century, uses her computer to find and sell used, out-of-print, and rare books all over the world.

COFFEE

Barnie's Coffee and Tea Company **407-629-0042**
Martin Kerns, Manager   **barniescoffee.com**
118 Park Avenue South
Winter Park 32789

This company was founded in Florida and was first on the Avenue with tantalizing coffee and tea flavors. By the cup or by the pound, Barnie's coffee and Barnie's tea are treats served up hot in the winter, and served up with ice to cool you in the summer. Look for the green awnings and let your nose lead the way.

DENTISTRY

Cosmetic & Restorative Dentistry **407-629-4077**
William Glover, III, D.M.D., P.A.
1320 South Orlando Avenue
Winter Park 32789

Veneers, Opalescence whitening, ceramic inlays and onlays, metal-free valplast partials, customized sports mouth guards, and implants. Dr. Glover has been in business locally for more than 15 years. He has discounts for senior citizens and Friday appointments for special procedures. 24-hour emergency coverage for Rollins College.

FLOWERS

Winter Park Florist **407-647-5014**
Debbie Ford   **800-874-7275**
519 Park Avenue South
Winter Park 32789

Debbie Ford, who has operated this wonderful florist shop for years, is the kind of person who knows just the right bouquet for every individual and every occasion. On special days of the season she and her staff work through the night to make sure every arrangement is perfect and every customer is delighted.

HARDWARE

Miller's Hardware 407-647-3316
Robert A. and Stephen Miller   **millers.doitbest.com**
143 Fairbanks Avenue
Winter Park 32789

Miller's is the oldest family-owned business in Winter Park, since Robert R. Miller moved here in 1939 and opened a five-and-dime on Park Avenue. In 1944 the family purchased the present property on Fairbanks for a paint store and in 1946 opened Miller's Hardware. Everyone in Winter Park shops at Miller's for paint, mulch, barbeque grills, bird feeders, nuts, bolts, alarm clocks, door mats and just about anything else for the home. The business is now run by the second and third generation of Millers.

INSURANCE

Helen Letter 407-740-6740
Allstate Insurance Company   **a070938@allstate.com**
Personal Financial Representative
400 West New England Avenue, Suite 1
Winter Park 32789

Helen has served Winter Park residents for eighteen years, so she and her staff are the go-to team to cover your auto, home, boat, business, and supplementary employee benefits. Financial services include life and long-term care insurance, mutual funds, annuities, and IRAs. An Exclusive Financial Specialist is available to put your retirement plan in perspective. Stop in for a free review and friendship!

JEWELRY AND ACCESSORIES

Columbia Jewelers 407-628-4461
Elizabeth Slade
102 Park Avenue South
Winter Park 32789

This has been a family-owned business since 1978, and the friendly atmosphere is evident from the moment you walk in the door. There is no pressure to buy because the stunning one-of-a-kind pieces sell themselves. Along with their fine diamond and gemstone jewelry, you will find lots of accessories, silver, watches, and estate jewelry. Or, let Elizabeth design something unique for you alone.

JEWELRY

Reynolds & Co. **407-645-2278**
David Reynolds   **reynoldsjewelers.com**
232 Park Avenue North
Winter Park 32789

David Reynolds is a second-generation jeweler on Park Avenue—his father started Reynolds & Co. back in 1974. The fine diamonds, gemstones, jewelry, timepieces, and estate jewelry are purchased and imported especially for you. All the work is backed by the kind of integrity it takes a third of a century to acquire. At Reynolds and Co. you can always expect service, quality and competitive prices.

Simmons Jewelers **407-644-3829**
Carole Simmons   **simmonsjewelers.com**
208 Park Avenue North
Winter Park 32789

Simmons has the exclusive line of Versace china, crystal, and flatware. They want to be your total diamond source—just as they have been for generations—so let the experts help you with engagement and wedding rings. They carry the platinum jewelry of Scott Kay, the number one choice of Today Show viewers. Simmons also carries estate jewelry, fine watches and accessories and specializes in expert jewelry and watch repair. You would expect no less from a family-owned business that has been on "The Avenue" since 1963.

LINENS

Luxe Linens **407-644-7677**
Ellen Prague
535 Park Avenue North – In the courtyard at Brandywine Square
Winter Park 32789

"Elegant essentials for luxurious living." Here you'll find a heaven of Egyptian cotton sheets, embroidered pillowcases, and French lace. Soft spa robes vie for your attention with quilted duvet covers and tablecloths handmade in Portugal. Imagine an English country house or a farmhouse in Tuscany and these linens would be there.

NEEDLEWORK

The Black Sheep **407-644-0122**
Caro Bradshaw   **800-641-0122**
128 Park Avenue South
Winter Park 32789

The Black Sheep has been on Park Avenue for nearly 30 years, and entering it is like entering a candy store for needle workers. There are hand-painted canvases, Persian wool yarns in every hue and color, knitting yarns, counted cross-stitch books and exquisite works of needlepoint art by celebrated designers. Group classes and personal instruction always available.

PHYSICIANS AND SURGEONS

Winter Park Plastic Surgery **407-645-2007**
J. Barry Boyd M.D. Board Certified **800-766-0225**
132 Benmore Drive **Naturallook.md**
Winter Park 32792

Listed as a Top Doctor in the U.S. with over 20 years of experience, Dr. J. Barry Boyd can refine your natural look. Quality care in a safe, private setting; including facial, breast, body contouring, hair restoration, skin and vein care. The 3,200-square-foot surgical facility is AAAASF certified, and staffed with the highest quality surgical staff, including M.D. Anesthesiologists for your safety. Meet with Dr. Boyd for a complimentary consultation, including a facility tour, to discuss your needs and wishes.

REAL ESTATE

Nancy Bagby, Realtor **407-644-1234 ex.123**
Fannie Hillman & Associates, Inc. **800-283-6235**
205 West Fairbanks **nancy@fanniehillman.com**
Winter Park 32789

Nancy Bagby is the name you will want when buying or selling real estate in the Winter Park, Maitland or Orlando area. She has resided in Winter Park and Maitland for the past 30 years and has been the top producer for Fannie Hillman & Associates for the past 15 years. Nancy knows the community from years of serving it and selling it.

Joan Cross, Realtor **407-629-8881**
Signature GMAC Real Estate™ **800-462-4906**
147 West Lyman Avenue **jcross@signaturerealty.net**
Winter Park 32789 **joanwcross@aol.com**

Joan Cross has made the Winter Park/Orlando area her home and workplace for many years and that gives her the expertise to give you service that sets her apart from the rest of the crowd. She keeps you informed and involved as she helps you find or sell a home for just the right value. With experience, integrity, and a personal touch, she daily lives her GMAC motto: "Service you Deserve from People You Trust!"

Tom Martin, Realtor **407-628-3010**
Vice President **800-821-0256**
Watson Realty Winter Park **Tommartin@watson-realty.com**
1720 Lee Road
Winter Park 32789

Watson is one of the largest independently owned real estate firms in the country. The Winter Park office serves not only the luxurious Winter Park market, it also serves Orlando, Maitland, Longwood and all other Central Florida neighborhoods of interest to you. Watson Realty uses the latest technology for both buyer and seller, to provide the Legendary Quality of Service that produces real results. Se habla Espanol!

Re/Max 200 Realty **407-629-6330**
Ronald Acker   **800-458-6863**
954 South Orlando Avenue   **racker@remax.net**
Winter Park 32789

There are more than 70 agents at Re/Max 200 Realty, and this customer service resulted in nearly 2000 satisfied homeowners this past year. To sell your home or assist you in purchasing, this professional staff is always there for you. They understand that this is a significant investment for you and your family. "Call us," says Ron Acker, Broker Owner (Rollins College '64).

Mark Squires & Mick Wetnight . . . . **407-256-6677** (Mark)
Realtor/Brokers   **407-629-4446** (Mick)
Coldwell Banker Residential Real Estate Inc.   **mickwetnight.realtor.com**
400 Park Avenue South, Suite 210
Winter Park 32789

Mick and Mark are well known in the Winter Park area for their top-of-the-line properties. You can count on them when you are looking for luxury homes, superior new construction, and prestigious lakefront property in "Olde" Winter Park, College Park and Maitland.

The Winter Park Land Company **407-644-2900**
Pitt Warner, Broker   **800-224-0003**
122 Park Avenue South   **winterparkland.com**
Winter Park 32789   **pwarner@winterparkland.com**

This company is the descendant of the original Winter Park Company, established in 1885 by the men who founded the city. Re-organized as The Winter Park Land Company in 1904, it now handles residential and commercial sales and service and operates as a traditional real estate brokerage. A great place to go to find the home just for you in Winter Park.

RESTAURANTS

Blackfin **407-691-4653**
Eric Kovar   **blackfinseafood.com**
460 North Orlando Avenue – Winter Park Village
Winter Park 32789

Blackfin became a hot spot the minute it opened its doors. The menu of just-caught fruits-of-the-sea changes daily, and the restaurant has received rave reviews. Opened by local entrepreneurs, led by Eric Kovar, Blackfin creates a cozy ambience inside and offers covered dining outside. If it's entertainment you're looking for, Blackfin is known for top local live music Wednesday through Saturday. Please call for daily specials and reservations.

Brandywine's Delicatessen 407-647-0055

Johnny and Kathleen Frankenberger
505 Park Avenue North, Suite 111
In Brandywine Square
Winter Park 32789

This family-owned restaurant has prospered for more than three decades on Park Avenue and its reputation guarantees you affordable quality and stress-free service.The menu board enables you to choose your favorite deli treats including turkey, roast beef, and ham cooked on the premises, and salads prepared daily. Tables indoors and out. Catering available for business meetings. One block north of the Morse Museum.

Park Plaza Gardens 407-645-2475

319 Park Avenue South **ParkPlazaGardens.com**
Winter Park 32789 **Mail@parkplazagardens.com**

This beautiful restaurant has been delighting local patrons and winning culinary awards and recognition since 1979. Its atrium style garden dining room lets the sun shine on your table as you sit in the coolness of the air conditioning and tantalize your palate with a range of luncheon offerings. At night the room becomes a setting for leisurely, romantic dinners from a menu that has earned it the title: "Central Florida's Most Popular Restaurant."

Le Restaurant Du Parc 407-647-4469
Maison des Crepes

The Heydel Family
348 Park Avenue North – In The Hidden Garden
Winter Park 32789

Here is a double treat: two restaurants in one, with kitchens headed by Lionel and G. Heydel, chefs and owners. They've received rave reviews for "artistry of the highest caliber" and "simple dishes done simply perfectly." Try their French cooking/wine pairings classes that end with a French feast. Special dining rates for groups of more than 10.

Ruth's Chris Steak House 407-622-2444

Lanette Jarvis **winterpark@ruthschris.com**
610 North Orlando Avenue – Winter Park Village
Winter Park 32789

"When it absolutely, positively has to be a great meal." USDA Prime Beef, seafood, and chicken. Beautiful, elegant décor, without the stuffy feeling. You can always expect exquisite service at this legendary restaurant.

Ristorante Trastevere 407-628-1277
"The Heart of Rome" members.aol.com/ristrastevere
Eydie Weinstein Ristrastevere@aol.com
Naomi Weinstein
400 South Orlando Avenue
Winter Park 32789

This restaurant was voted "Orlando's most romantic" and the wonderful news is that it is right here in Winter Park! Enjoy award-winning Italian cuisine indoors in a unique, old-wine-cellar atmosphere, or relax outside in a private Italian courtyard. Exquisite dining, fine wines, and the very best service. Don't miss the fabulous Sunday brunch!

SHOPPING CENTERS

Winter Park Village 407-571-2700
Leslie Sanguinet-Wright shopwinterparkvillage.com
480 North Orlando Avenue lsanguinetwright@castosoutheast.com
Winter Park 32789

Winter Park Village is the newest shopping center development in Winter Park. When you visit the Village you can shop at the many unique stores, take in a movie at the 20-screen Regal Cinemas, or dine at one of the Village's many fine restaurants. Visit the Web site to see all that Winter Park Village has to offer.

STATIONERY AND ACCESSORIES

Maureen H. Hall Stationery and Invitations 407-629-6999
Maureen Hall hallinvitations@aol.com
116 Park Avenue South–Greeneda Court
Winter Park 32789

This is the store for fine paper! Nestled in Greeneda Court (behind Barnie's Coffee) you will find the coziest shop with a complete assortment of custom wedding invitations and stationery, fabulous party invitations and more. A source for Crane's and William Arthur, elegant locals have been depending on Maureen Hall since 1977. Once you discover this divine spot you will definitely join its legions of devoted fans!

The Paper Shop 407-644-8700
Ellen Prague sales@papershop.com
545 Park Avenue North
Winter Park 32789

This store, a fixture on Park Avenue for 20 years, has a loyal following. Ellen Prague travels the world to find the kind of stationery and note cards that make letters and invitations a pleasure to send. She also sells beautiful pens; Filofax notebooks and inserts; journals; photo albums; and a fabulous selection of objets d'art and unique gifts. Winter Park shops here for its party and wedding invitations.

WORSHIP

All Saints' Episcopal Church **407-647-3413**
The Reverend H. David Wilson
338 East Lyman Avenue
Winter Park 32789

Founded in 1883, All Saints' continues to thrive as one of the most active churches in the community. Its Healing Ministry brings in Christians from all over the world. Its many activities, from Bible study groups to weekly fellowship suppers help involve its members in outreach as well as community building. Pioneer Mary Brown attended here and a window she dedicated to her missionary father can still be found in the vestry.

First Congregational Church UCC **407-647-2416**
Rev. Bryan G. Fulwider, Senior Minister **fccwp.org**
225 South Interlachen **fccwp@fccwp.org**
Winter Park 32789

"A traditional and nurturing church celebrating God's grace through reason, education, diversity, inclusion, and social justice." The oldest church in Winter Park, established in 1884 under Rev. Dr. Edward P. Hooker, counted many town founders among its early members. When the Congregational Church established Rollins College in 1885, Dr. Hooker became its first president. The present church building replaced the original structure in 1924.

St. Margaret Mary Catholic Church **407-647-3392**
Rev. Richard M. Walsh, Pastor **stmargaretmary.org**
526 Park Avenue North
Winter Park 32789

St. Margaret Mary Catholic Church stands in the heart of Winter Park's downtown business district and witnesses to the faith life of this community. The original church was built in 1924. Continued growth necessitated the building of the present structure. Dedicated in 1969, it was a trendsetter in contemporary church architecture. Prayerful celebrations, community building, and compassionate service are hallmarks of this vibrant church's congregation.

BIBLIOGRAPHY

Audubon Society Field Guide to Florida Knopf 1998

A Pilgrimage of Windows to God by Anna Mavor,
Published by All Saints Church, Winter Park , Florida 1974

Blackman's History of Orange County Florida by William Fremont Blackman, E.O.
Painter Printing Company, De Land, Florida 1927

Chronological History of Winter Park by Claire Leavett MacDowell,
Orange Press 1950

City of Winter Park 2001 Welcome Book published by the Public Relations and
Communications Division of The City of Winter Park

The Diaries of Mary E. Brown, 1876-1898, unpublished, available for research at the
Winter Park Public Library Reference Department, Winter Park History Section

The Episcopal Church in Winter Park, Florida by Stetson Conn, published by All Saints
Church of Winter Park 1984

Florida Indians and the Invasion from Europe by Jerald Melanich,
Gainesville University Press 1995

Historic Winter Park, A Driving Tour compiled by the Junior League of Orlando-Winter
Park, Inc. 1980

Hammond's Nature Atlas of America by E.L. Jordan, illustrations by Walter Ferguson,
C.S. Hammond and Company, New York, New York 1952 (out of print)

Millennium Memories, The National Bank of Commerce 1999

Park Avenue Walking Tour compiled by the Winter Park
Historical Association, Inc. 2001

James Gamble Rogers II: Residential Architecture in Winter Park by Debra L. Alderson
and Patrick W. McClane, (self-published, no date)

**A Side Walk with the Art Festival: A Collector's Encyclopedia of the Winter Park
Sidewalk Art Festival** by Elizabeth Bradley Bentley, The Winter Park Sidewalk Art Festival
1979

Tales of Winter Park edited by Hope Strong, Jr., Rollins Press 1984

The Timucuas by Jerald Melanich, Oxford University Press 1996

What's Cookin' in Florida Bev-Ron Publishing Company, Kansas City, Missouri, March 1967

Winter Park Portrait: The Story of Winter Park and Rollins College by Richard N.
Campen, West Summit Press, Beachwood, Ohio 1987

ACKNOWLEDGMENTS

Many thanks to: Gertrude F. Laframboise and Department of College Archives and Special Collections, Olin Library Rollins College; The Winter Park Historical Association, Inc., Mrs. Marianne Popkins, Executive Director; Mr. John Tiedtke for his review of the material; The Winter Park Public Library, Robert G. Melanson, Director and Winter Park History Reference Department, Mr. Dean Padgett, Winter Park History Librarian, with special thanks to Kristin Kitchen; Mrs. Peggy Strong; Mr. Dave Marsh, WESH-TV Meteorologist; Dr. Joe Nassif, Producing Director, Winifred M. Warden, Chair of Theatre Arts and Dance, Rollins College; Mr. Rick Frazee, General Manager of the Best Western Mt. Vernon Inn; Mr. Russell Hughes of Orlando; Mr. Peter Schreyer, Executive Director, Crealdé School of Art; Ms. Fairolyn Livingston for her help on the issues facing West Winter Park; Mr. John H. Rogers, President, Rogers, Lovelock & Fritz, Inc.; Mrs. Flora Twachtman for her gracious tour of "Eastbank"; Mrs. Lydia Gardner, Clerk of the Courts for Orange County, Mrs. Carolyn Bird, Miss Lisa Mills, and Mr. Tim Brown for their help "test-driving" the Driving Tour; Mrs. Tim Gould, and Ms. Diane Rinkes for their kind help in proofreading. Very special thanks to Mrs. Evelyn Pettit, of Brandywine Books, for her prodigious work editing my manuscript.

All the old postcards used in this book are from the collections of Mr. Rick Frazee and Mr. Russell Hughes. I owe them both an enormous debt for their gracious loans.

The poster images and photographs of the Winter Park Sidewalk Art Festival are used with the permission of the WPSAF.

The images of Tiffany windows and lamps are used with the permission of the Charles Hosmer Morse Museum of American Art.

The images of the Polasek Museum are used with the permission of the Albin Polasek Museum and Sculpture Garden.

The images from the collection of the Cornell Fine Arts Museum are used with the permission of Rollins College.

The images of the Bach Festival are used with the permission of the Bach Festival Society.

The historic photos are used with the permission of the Department of College Archives and Special Collections, Olin Library Rollins College, and the Winter Park Public Library.

None of these images is to be used or reproduced in any fashion without the express permission of the aforementioned organizations.

POST.OFFICE. WINTER PARK. FLA.